Name Your Child

49

22/12

Name Your Child

A handy guide for puzzled parents

Eric Partridge

Evans Brothers Limited London

Published by Evans Brothers Limited,
Montague House, Russell Square,
London, W.C.1

Originally published in this shorter form in 1959
by Hamish Hamilton and revised and enlarged for
the first paperback edition 1968
9th printing 1981

Set in 9 on 11 point Univers and printed in
Great Britain by Cox & Wyman Limited, Reading
ISBN 0 237 44417 8

PRA 7135

Preface

A small dictionary of given or Christian names seems to be called for.

Etymologies or word-origins have been kept to a minimum. That minimum is unavoidable, for, by explaining the meaning of the name, it saves the parents from making some very unwise—perhaps ridiculous—choice. Remember: it is the child who carries the burden of an unsuitable name; he's saddled with it for life.

List of abbreviations

A.S. Anglo-Saxon. The same as O.E.: some writers prefer the one, some the other.
Apperson. G. L. Apperson, English Proverbs and Provincial Phrases, 1929.
Benedictines. The Book of Saints, by the Benedictine Monks of St. Augustine's Abbey, 1921.
Blakeney. E. H. Blakeney, A Smaller Classical Dictionary, 1910.
C. Century: e.g., C19, the 19th Century; C14-20, during the 14th-20th centuries.
ca. About (in dates).
cf. Compare.
'Christian'. A Christian or given name.
d. Died (in).
Dawson. A Book of the Saints, by Lawrence Dawson, 1908.
e.g. For example.
f. Feminine.
Fr. French.
Ger. German; Germanic.
Gr. Greek.
Harvey. Sir Paul Harvey, The Oxford Companion to English Literature.
Heb. Hebrew.
ibid. In the same 'authority'.
i.e. That is.
It. Italian.
Jack and Jill. Ernest Weekley, Jack and Jill, 1939.
L. Latin.
Lit. Literally; literal.
Loughead. Flora Loughead, Given Names, 1934.
m. Masculine.
M.E. Middle English.
O.E. Old English.
O.E.D. The Oxford English Dictionary.
q.v. Which see. Plural: qq.v.
Reaney. P. H. Reaney, A Dictionary of British Surnames, 1958.
Sp. Spanish.
Swan. Helena Swan, Christian Names, 1905.
Webster. Webster's New International Dictionary, 2nd edition, 1934.
Weekley. Ernest Weekley, An Etymological Dictionary of Modern English, 1921.
Weekley's Romance of Names, Surnames, W. & N. Respectively his The Romance of
Names, 1914, Surnames, 1916; and Words and Names, 1932.
Withycombe. E. G. Withycombe, The Oxford Dictionary of English Christian Names, 1945.
Yonge, Charlotte Yonge, History of Christian Names, revised ed., 1884.

A

Aaron Perhaps from the Hebrew for '(a) light', but probably of Egyptian origin (Withycombe), this is a Biblical patriarch's name.

Abbey A diminutive of **Abigail.**

Abe A mainly American diminutive of **Abraham.**

Abel This pleasantly manly name is derived from the Hebrew (literally, vanity).

Abigail This Biblical name means 'father's joy'—or something of the sort. Diminutives: **Abbey** and **Gail.**

Abie See **Aby.**

Abner Lit. 'father of light' or 'my father is light', this m. name derives from the Hebrew.

Abraham The greatest of the Biblical patriarchs was originally called 'Abram (father of height or elevation), which was changed by Divine appointment into Abraham (father of a multitude), foretelling the numerous and enduring offspring that have descended from him'. (Yonge.)

Aby or Abie An American pet-form of **Abraham.**

Ada This f. name is obscure in origin. 'I conjecture that Ada is short for Adela' (Weekley in **Jack and Jill**). Contrast:

Adah A Hebrew name, denotes an ornament.

Adam This fine old name means, in Hebrew, 'man', itself from Heb. adamah, red earth. It lost, centuries ago, its Semitic connotations.

Addie, Addy Pet-name forms, in Devon of **Audrey,** elsewhere of **Adelina, Adeline,** and:

Adela Of Teutonic origin: 'noble'.

Adelaide Of Teutonic origin: 'nobility'.

Adelina or Adeline Lengthens **Adela.**

Adolf, Adolph, m. The anglicized forms of:

Adolphus From the Teutonic for 'noble wolf'. Now to be avoided, for it ranks with **Algernon** and **Cuthbert** as comically pompous.

Adrian This attractive m. name comes from the L. **Adrianus or Hadrianus** (cf. the Roman emperor Hadrian).

Adriana the f. form of Adrian. Rare in the Commonwealth it survives mainly in its Fr. form **Adrienne.**

Afra or Aphra perhaps shortens **Aphrodite.**

Agatha A responsible name, for in **Gr.** it means 'good'. Its diminutive, **Aggie,** is perhaps to be avoided.Cf.:

Agnes derives from a Greek word signifying 'pure'. Diminutives: **Aggie** and even **Ag.**

Aileen occasionally **Ailleen.** An Irish 'shape' of **Helen.**

Ailie A Scottish contraction of **Alison.**

Ailsa A Scottish form of Elsa.

Al A mainly American diminutive of **Albert.** Also a diminutive of **Alfred** and **Alexander.**

Alan, Allan, Allen; Welsh **Alun.** It comes, by way of French, from the Medieval Latin **Alanus,** of unknown origin; perhaps originally the name of a tribe or a people.

Alaric m. This English form derives from L. **Alaricus,** itself from a Germanic name meaning 'all-ruler'.

Alastair, Alaster, Alistair, Alisteir, Alister Scottish contractions of **Alexander.**

Alban As an English Christian name, **Alban** comes from St Alban, that Roman soldier who, the first British martyr, suffered martyrdom near what is now St Albans.

Alberga f. A somewhat rare name that probably derives from the Teutonic word for 'noble'.

Albert From A. S. **Aethelbeorht,** nobly bright.

Alberta, Albertina, Albertine These are f. derivatives of **Albert.**

Alda f. An ancient German name, meaning 'old'.

Aldis, Aldus, Aldous The m. counterparts of **Alda.**

Alec; Alick. Scottish diminutives of **Alexander.** Cf. ı

Alex Properly an English contraction (cf. **Alec**) of, but nowadays occasionally used as a substitute for, **Alexander.** Also a diminutive of **Alexandra, Alexandrina, Alexia, Alexis.**

Alexander Originally a complimentary byname ('helper, or defender, of men') given to Greek Paris 'for his courage in repelling robbers from the flocks. It was afterwards a regular family name of the kings of Macedon, he who gave it fame being the third who bore it. So much revered as well as feared was this mighty conqueror, that his name still lives in proverb and song throughout the East'. (Yonge).

Alexandra The f. form of the preceding. A royal name; its original diminutive, **Alexandrina.**

Alexia Sometimes a contraction of **Alexandra;** sometimes a variant of **Alicia.**

Alexis An English contraction of **Alexander.** Now somewhat rare as a m. name; but occasionally f. in C20.

Alfred From a Teutonic word meaning 'elf in council', hence 'a wise counsellor'. It was the fame of King Alfred which popularized the name in England.

Alfreda The f. of **Alfred.**

Algernon This aristocratic name has a slightly comic origin, for it means 'whiskered'.

Algy Endearment of the preceding. Glorified in: 'Algy met a bear. The bear was bulgy. The bulge was Algy.'

Alice, Alicia The former is an English, the latter a Latin handling, of Gr. aletheia, truth.

Alick See **Alec.**

Aline Contracts **Adeline.**

Alison A Scottish diminutive of **Alice**; -on is a French suffix, present also in **Marion.**

Alistair, Alisteir, Alister See **Alastair.**

Alix f. From **Alicia.**

Allan, Allen, Variations of **Alan,** q.v.

Allie, Ally The usual diminutive of **Aileen** and **Alice.**

Alma f. This name has four origins: a Russian place-name, popularized by the Battle of Alma, 1854; L. alma (fair or kindly girl); Celtic for 'all good'; and Hebrew for 'maiden'.

Almeric, Almerick In Teutonic, lit. a 'work-ruler'.

Almira An import from Spain, the word simply meaning 'a woman of Almeira' or Almeria.

Aloysius m. ML **Aloisius,** of the same origin as **Louis.** It has five syllables and, in predominantly Protestant countries, it is a Catholic name.

Alphonso m. A slightly discredited name, of which the It. and Sp. form is **Alfonso.**

Althea This pleasant name derives from Gr., where it means 'healthy' or 'wholesome'.

Alwyn is a variant of **Aylwin.**

Alys A fanciful spelling of **Alice.**

Amabel, Amabella A mostly American variant of **Amy,** probably on the analogy of **Annabel, Annabella.**

Amaryllis f. 'Refreshing stream' in the Gr.

Amber f. With this mainly American name, not general before C20, cf. **Coral** and **Emerald** and **Pearl.**

Ambrose m. A 'Christian' of Gr. origin; its sense, 'immortal'.

Amelia An English offshoot from **Emily**.

Amias, Amyas, perhaps derives from the surname **Amias,** '(man of) Amiens'.

Amice, Amecia, Amicia Variants of **Amy**.

Amos from Heb. for 'borne (by God)' is a friendly name.

Amy If one remembers its origin—Fr. **Aimée,** from L. amata (a woman beloved)—it assumes a vesture of charm.

Amyas See **Amias**.

Amyot means 'loved by God'.

Anastasia occasionally **Anstace** or **Anstice**; masculine, **Anastasius** Lit., 'she or he who awakes or arises'.

Andrea is the f. of:

Andrew From **Andreas** in Syriac Gr., it derives from Gr. aner, genitive andros, a man. **Andreas,** one of the foremost of the Apostles, was martyred at Patras, whence, in C4, some of his relics went to Scotland and thus made of St Andrew's the Metropolitan see. St Andrew, patron saint of Scotland, was also its 'knightly champion'.

Andy A contraction of **Andrew**.

Aneurin m. This Welsh name means 'truly (a'n) golden' (eurin).

Angela and its derivative **Angelica** mean 'the angelic girl or woman'. **Angela** originated as the f. of Gr. angelos, an angel, but in Classical Gr. a messenger.

Angelina A diminutive of **Angela**.

Angie (pronounced **Anjee**). A diminutive of **Angela, Angelica, Angelint**.

Angus Originally **Oengus,** it was popular in Ireland and then, by migration, in Scotland; Modern Irish **Aonghus,** Gaelic

Aonghas. Lit., it means 'unique choice'. (**Alexander, Angus, Andrew, Donald, Hamish, Ian** are perhaps the most popular of Scottish m. Christian names.)

Anita A diminutive of **Ann(a)**.

Ann See **Anne**.

Anna The original form of **Anne**.

Annabel, Annabella, derive from **Amabel,** influenced by **Anna**. Pet-name: **Bella**.

Anne, Ann The latter is distinctively English form of the originally Fr. **Anne,** from Gr. **Anna,** from Heb. **Chaanah** or **Hannah** (grace). Pet-form: **Nan**.

Annette is, originally, a Fr. diminutive of **Anne**.

Annie The pleasantly familiar form of **Ann(e)**.

Annis See **Annys**.

Annot f. Mainly Scottish. Usually a diminutive of **Agnes** or of ;

Annys or **Annis** A variation of **Agnes**.

Anselm From the Teutonic for 'divine helmet'.

Anstace f. **Anstice,** f. See **Anastasia**.

Ansty A contraction of **Anastasius**.

Anthea In Gr., '(a lady of) flowers'.

Anthony; Antony The superfluous h seems to have been introduced by the Dutch and the French. **Antony** comes from L. **Antonius,** which some authorities explain as 'inestimable' and others as 'strength'. Diminutive **Tony**.

Antonia The f. of **Antonius,** hence of **Antony**.

Antony See **Anthony**

Aphra See **Afra**.

April See **Averil.**

Arabella 'I conjecture that Arabella was an amalgamation of this name (**Annabel** or **Annabella**) with Orable' or Orabella, surviving in the surname Orbell and deriving from L. orabilis, 'yielding to prayer' (**Jack and Jill**). Pet-name: **Bella.**

Archibald From the Teutonic for 'truly bold', its earliest form being **Ercanbald.** Diminutive: **Archie.**

Arianwen f. A Welsh name from a word meaning 'silver'.

Arnold From the Teutonic **Arnwald** (eagle-strong).

Art A diminutive, in England reputed to be vulgar, of ï

Arthur Of completely unknown origin, it is a very distinguished name, referring both to King Arthur and his Knights of the Round Table and to Arthur Wellesley, Duke of Wellington. (See especially Withycombe and Reaney.)

Artie A diminutive of **Arthur** and **Arthurine.**

Asa m. Rare in Britain but common in America, **Asa** comes from the Hebrew and signifies 'God healeth'.

Asta f. Somewhat rare in England, it may be a contraction of **Augusta.**

Astrid f. This Norwegian name ('divine strength') has, since ca. 1920, gained a footing in England.

Athanasius Gr. **Athanasios,** 'undying, immortal'.

Atty m. An Irish name, perhaps from the Celtic for 'high' (cf. **Arthur**).

Aubrey has come to England, via France, from Old German **Albirich,** lit. 'elf-rule', hence 'elf ruler'. Cf. **Alfred.**

Auda f., means 'rich'.

Audrey occasionally **Audry.** A contraction of A.S. **Etheldreda** ('noble might').

Augusta The f. of **Augustus**. Diminutive: **Gussy**.

Augustin, Augustine A diminutive of:

Augustus Although now, in the Commonwealth, held somewhat pompous, it is an imperial name; it appears pretentious only when it is set in juxtaposition to **Bill** and **Jack** and **Tom**. It derives from L. augere ('to increase'). Pet-form: **Gus**.

Aurelia f. 'Golden', i.e. goldilocks, from L. aurum, gold.

Aurora From L. for 'dawn', Aurora was originally the Roman goddess of dawn.

Austin or **Austen** An English contraction of **Augustin**.

Averil, Averyl, Averilla Meaning 'Wild-boar battle-maid', it has a male companion in **Everard**.

Avice f.; occasionally **Avicia**. Ultimately from Ger. **Hedwig,** 'war-refuge'.

Avis f. From L. avis, a bird.

Avril is the Fr. for April.

Avvy Endearment of the four preceding names.

Awdrey or **Awdrey** A variant of **Audrey**.

Aylmer m. probably derives from the A.-S. **Aethelmaer,** nobly famous'.

Aylwin m. Germanic for 'noble friend'.

B

Bab, Babs Scottish **Babie** Diminutives of **Barbara.**

Baldwin Lit. 'a bold friend'.

Balthasar m., is a Gr. form of the Biblical **Belshazzar,** one of the Three Holy Kings.

Barbara (Diminutives: **Bab, Babie, Babs, Bar.**) The word is the f. of barbaros, a stranger—a term scornfully applied by the Greeks to all who did not speak their mellifluous tongue.

Barnaby Like the rare **Barnabas,** it derives from the Hebrew and means 'son of exhortation'.

Barnard, Barnett English variants of **Bernard** (Italian and Spanish **Bernardo**), they imply 'the resolution, firmness, of a bear'.

Barney, Barny A diminutive of **Barnaby** and **Barnard.**

Barry An Irish m. name, from the Celtic for 'spear-like' or 'good spearman.'

Bart A diminutive of **Bartholomew.**

Bartle A diminutive of **Bartlemy.**

Bartholomew Heb., 'son of **Talmai** (abounding in furrows)', so presumably the name was given first to a ploughman. It has many religious associations.

Bartie A diminutive of **Bartholomew;** also of **Bartram.**

Bartlemy An Anglicizing of **Bartholomew.**

Bartlet An English contraction of **Bartholomew.**

Bartley An Irish contraction of **Bartholomew.**

Bartram English; **Barthram,** Scottish. Lit., 'bright raven' (Teutonic), they form a group with German **Bertram** and French **Bertrand.**

Basil In Gr., it means 'a King'.

Basty is the usual diminutive of **Sebastian**.

Bathsheba From Heb., it means either 'daughter of the oath' or 'seventh daughter'.

Bea pronounced **Bee**. Diminutive of **Beatrice**.

Beatie An English diminutive, like **Tricia, Trix, Trissy, Trixy,** of :.

Beatrice, Beatrix The latter is the original; **Beatrice** is now the usual form in England and even in Italy. In L., it is 'blessed'.

Becky A pet-form of **Rebecca**.

Bede A Teutonic name, meaning 'prayer', it is now rarely heard except among Catholics.

Belinda Although, in It., she is a serpent, **Belinda** has been popular in English literature and probably owes something to Fr. belle, beautiful.

Bell, Bella, Belle Contractions of **Isabel** or **Isabella,** the Fr. **Isabelle** obviously being party to the act; **Bella** is also a diminutive of **Annabella** and **Arabella**.

Benedict From L. benedictus (blessèd).

Benjamin Heb. 'son of the right hand'. It owes much of its popularity to the lovable nature of the youngest of Joseph's brethren. Diminutives: **Benjy, Benny, Ben.**

Bennet A pet-name form of Benedict, of which it is a typically English contraction.

Berenice Originally **Pherenice**, a Macedonian name, it derives from Gr. and, there, it means 'victory-bringing'.

Bernard (Cf. Barnard.) From biornhard, 'having the resolution, or courage, of a bear'.

Bernie Pet-form of **Bernard**.

Bert A diminutive of **Albert**; rarely of **Bertram** or **Bertrand**.

Bertha In Teutonic languages, 'the bright one' or 'the shining one'; cf. the first element in **Bertram**.

Bertie A diminutive of **Albert**; also of **Bertha, Bertrand** and :

Bertram Like the next, it is equivalent to **Bartram**. Teutonic, it means 'bright raven'.

Bertrand See the preceding. Originally the Fr. form. Its heroic associations spring from the fame of Bertrand du Guesclin, the C14 champion of France.

Beryl A 'jewel-name': cf. **Pearl** and **Ruby**.

Bess, Bessie English diminutives of **Elizabeth**; cf. **Beth, Betsy, Betty**.

Beth A diminutive of both **Elizabeth** and :

Bethia, Bethiah f. From Heb. bith-jah, 'daughter, i.e. servant, of Jehovah'. It is American and rural English.

Betsy An English diminutive of **Elizabeth**.

Betta Originally and mainly a German contraction and diminutive of **Elizabeth**: cf. **Betty**. The C20 prefers **Bette**.

Bettrys The Welsh form of **Beatrice**.

Betty A diminutive of **Elizabeth**: cf. **Bess** (q.v.), **Beth, Betsy**.

Bevis 'It appears to be simply the "bull", Old Fr. Bueves being a common name in epic' (**Jack and Jill**).

Biddulph In A.S., 'commanding wolf'.

Biddy An Irish contraction of **Bridget**.

Bill A contraction and transformation of **William**. Its own diminutive is **Billy**.

Blaise Properly the Fr. original of **Blase** or **Blaze**. Probably from L. blaesus, splay-footed.

Blanche occasionally **Blanch**. Lit., 'white'.

Blase, Blaze English forms of **Blaise.**

Bob A diminutive of **Robert**: cf. the obsolete **Hob** and the obsolescent **Rob**; also **Bobbie** and **Robin.**

Boniface From the L. for 'a well-doer'.

Boris Either from the Hungarian for 'a stranger' or, more probably, from the Russian for 'a fight'.

Boyd In Celtic, 'yellow'.

Bram A Dutch and, hence, American contraction of **Abraham,** q.v., but often used in ignorance of its origin.

Bran From the Celtic for 'a raven', this m. name is rare outside of Wales and the Scottish Highlands.

Brand A mainly and originally Scandinavian name (lit., 'a flame; hence, a sword-blade'), which is the m. of the next.

Brenda Probably the f. of **Brand**. 'The sword figures in northern and German nomenclature as Brand', as Charlotte Yonge remarks.

Brian, Bryan Lit., 'strong'. It has long been a favourite, both in Brittany—as **Brien**—and in Ireland.

Bride A mainly Scottish contraction of **Bridget.**

Bridget occasionally **Bridgit, Brigid** or **Brigit.** (Properly **Brighid.**) Lit., 'lofty' or 'august'. It is, of all 'Christians', the most frequently given in Ireland: this popularity results directly from the fame of the late C5-early 6 virgin saint, who was born of Christian parents at Fouchard in Louth.

Bronwen f. In Celtic, 'white-breasted'. It is a Welsh name.

Bruce m., was originally, as it still is, a Scottish surname drawn from **Brieux** in France.

Brunhild, Brunehilda, Brunhilda In Ger. the word must signify 'the breastplate maid of battle'.

Bruno Mostly a Ger. name; lit., 'brown'.

Brush A very English contraction of **Ambrose.**

Bryan A variant of **Brian**.

Bunty is an affectionate, sportive personification, either of the dialectal bunty, (of a person) 'dumpy—i.e., short and stout', or of **Bunty**, a pet-name for a lamb.

C

Cadell A Welsh m. 'Christian'. In Celtic, it means 'strength in war'. Now somewhat rare as a font-name.

Cadogan Welsh m. Here the first element is the Celtic cath or cad, war, a battle or a defence; the second element is obscure,

Cadwallader Welsh m.: cf. the preceding pair of names and **Cadwallon** It signifies 'battle-arranger'.

Cadwallon Welsh m. For the **Cad-**, see preceding trio of names; the -wallon may stand for 'lord'.

Caesar The name appeared first in the Julian gens or clan, nearly 200 years before Julius Caesar. Probably from the fact that the first Caesar had an abundance of hair (L. caesaries); Julius Caesar, oddly enough, was bald-headed.

Caintigern f. An Irish name: in Erse, 'fair lady'.

Cal The diminutive of **Calliope, Calypso, Calvin,** and:

Caleb In Heb., 'a dog'. In Judges, Caleb was the staunch and faithful spy, who, of the 600,000 persons that had come out of Egypt, alone went with Joshua into the Promised Land.

Calliope In Gr., '(she of the) beautiful voice'.

Calvin Mostly American, it commemorates the great Protestant reformer (1509-64). Etymologically, it is a diminutive of L. calvus, 'bald'.

Camilla L. f. name, from camilla, a noble maiden serving in a temple.

Candida A L. name, meaning 'white': cf. **Blanche.**

Cara f. Mostly an Irish name, it comes from the Celtic for 'friend'. In C20 non-Irish use, there is often an allusion to It. cara (dear girl).

Caradoc m. 'Beloved' (Celtic).

Carey or **Cary** Properly a surname.

Carl The anglicized spelling of the originally Ger. **Karl,** which is the general Teutonic 'shape' of **Charles.**

Carlile Properly a surname, also in forms **Carlyle** and **Carlisle;** 'man of Carlisle'.

Carlo The Italian form (cf. Sp. **Carlos**) of **Charles,** this name is gaining ground in Britain and U.S.A. Cf. **Carl.**

Carmel, Carmela f. In Heb., 'vineyard' or 'fruitful field', the name is more frequent in Italy than in England.

Carmichael In Celtic, 'friend of Michael', with special reference to the Archangel Michael. Diminutive: **Car.**

Carol m. Either an adoption of Polish and Slovakian **Karol** or a shortening of L. **Carolus;** cf. the English equivalent: **Charles.** It is also the pet-form of **Carolina** or **Caroline,** and is often bestowed independently of these names.

Carola The direct f. of L. **Carolus** (see **Carol**).

Carolina, Caroline Originally Continental forms—the former, predominantly Italian—corresponding to Fr. and English **Charlotte,** itself the f. counterpart to **Charles.**

Carrie occasionally **Carry.** The usual diminutive of **Carola, Carolina** or **Caroline,** as **Chatty** and **Lottie** are of **Charlotte.**

Caspar usually **Casper.** From the Persian for 'horseman';
sometimes a variant of **Jasper.**

Cassandra In Gr., 'helper of men'. Pet-form: **Cass.**

Catharina, Catherine English forms of **Katharina, Katherine.**

Cathleen See **Kathleen.**

Cecil Ultimately from L. caecus, blind, it derives from the
Caecilian 'gens'; it serves as the m. of **Cecilia.** Pet-name: **Cec,**
pronounced **Sess.**

Cecilia (For origin, see **Cecil.**) The name owes its popularity
less to its connexions with Roman history than to the fame of
the virgin martyr, St Caecilia (died ca. 176).

Cecilie, Cecily English forms of the preceding.

Cedric arose from Scott's mistake for **Cerdic,** the name of the
first king of Wessex (d. 534).

Celia Derives from L. **Caelia,** itself from caelum, heaven:
'heavenly (girl)'.

Charis f. (The ch is hard, i.e. as kh.) The C19-20 form of:

Charissa From the Gr. for 'love', hence 'charity' (Faith, Hope, and
Charity).

Charity (For origin, see **Charissa.**) Charlotte Yonge is not to be
denied: 'It was reserved for Christianity to give the word its
higher sense. Charis, through the Latin caritas, grew to be the
Christian's Charity. . . . And it was thus that, after the
Reformation, Charity, (often) contracted into Cherry, became an
English Christian name.'

Charles Earliest as **Karl,** which in Teutonic languages means
'a man'. The form **Charles** seems to have been Fr.—from a
blending of **Karl** (become **Carl**) and its L. 'shape', **Carolus.**

Charlotte Probably from Fr. **Charlot,** the pet-name for **Charles.**

Charmian, Charmion Though from Gr. kharma, a (source of) joy,
delight, the ch is usually pronounced soft.

Chatty A very English transformation (at first, only an endearment) of **Charlotte**: cf., therefore, **Lottie (-y)**.

Chauncey or **Chauncy** Originally and strictly a surname, of French origin.

Cherry See **Charity**. It is often used with an underlying reference to the bloom and colour of the fruit.

Chloe (Pronounced cló-ee.) In Gr., 'a green and tender shoot'.

Chris Diminutive of **Christopher**, **Christina** (or **-e**), **Christabel**. Cf.:

Chrissie is the familiar form of **Christina** (and **-e**).

Christabel From Gr. khristos (L. **Christus**, the Anointed One) and L. bellus, f. bella, handsome.

Christian (Now rarely, though originally, f.) Direct from L. **Christianus**, a follower of Christ.

Christiana The f. of **Christian**.

Christie, Christy A diminutive of **Christopher**.

Christina Alternative for, and the original of, **Christine**. It is the f. diminutive of **Christus** (see **Christabel**).

Christine At first, it was rather Scottish (probably from France) than English, this mere variation of **Christina**.

Christopher In Gr., lit. 'Christ-bearing'. The St Christopher of legend and, less, the historic martyr popularized the name. Pet-names: **Chris** and **Kit**.

Chrystal or **Crystal**, f., is a jewel-name.

Cicero Seldom used in England; rather more often in U.S.A. After the great Roman orator and writer. In L., lit. 'vetch'; the first Cicero perhaps cultivated vetches.

Cicely, Cicily The latter probably deviates from the former, which in turn deviates from **Cecily**. Diminutives: **Cis** or **Sis; Cissie** or **Sissie**.

Ciprian, Cyprian m. In L., 'inhabitant of Cyprus'.

Clair, Clare m. Counterparts to:

Clara It is the f. of L. clarus, 'clear', hence 'renowned': cf. the origin of **Clarence**.

Clarence From L. clarens, the present participle of clarere, 'to be renowned'.

Claribel A derivative of **Clara**; probably on the model of **Christabel**.

Clarice Lit., 'making famous'; from L. clarus, 'renowned'. At first It., the name travelled to France and then to England Whence **Clarissa**.

Clarinda A fanciful f. name, from **Clara** or **Florinda**.

Clarissa See **Clarice**.

Clarrie The diminutive of **Clarence** and **Clara**.

Claud, Claude The English form of **Claudius**.

Claudia f. **Claudius**, m. From L. claudus, 'lame'. Both the f. and the m. names are famous in Roman history.

Claudian From **Claudianus**, a derivative of **Claudius**.

Claudine A Fr. form of **Claudia** adopted in England.

Claudius See **Claudia**.

Clem, Clemmie Diminutives of:

Clemence f. rare and mostly French, the usual English f. being **Clemency, Clement**, m. from L. **Clemens**, 'the merciful'. **Clement** is a favourite with the Popes of Rome.

Clementina A specifically English variation of:

Clementine Originally Ger. (**Klementine**: cf. Fr. **Clémentine**), but popularized in England and U.S.A. in C19, especially in the song, 'My Darling Clementine'. A feminine diminutive from L. clemens, mild, merciful.

Cleo The diminutive of:

Cleopatra In Gr., it means, 'glory, fame, of one's father'. Cleopatra. who died in 30 B.C. at the age of 39, was the last of the Ptolemies in Egypt, which, on her death, became a Roman province. Beautiful, charming, and wise ('serpent of old Nile'), she figures largely in European literature.

Clifford as a personal name, signifies 'dweller by a cliff' or 'dweller on a slope'.

Clifton is properly a surname. Diminutive: **Clif.**

Clive became a 'Christian' in honour of 'Clive of India' (1725-74), who won notable victories at Arcot and Plassey, 1751 and 1757. **Clive** comes from cliff.

Clo The diminutive of **Chloe** and of the next two names.

Clodagh is an Irish f. from a river name.

Clotilda, Clotilde The former is a mainly L., the latter a mainly Fr. name.

Colan m. A Cornish name, meaning 'a dove'.

Colbert m. In the Teutonic, 'cool brightness'; a French as well as an English name.

Colborn m. In Teutonic, 'a black bear'.

Colette This f. is properly Fr., but is gaining ground in post-war England. It corresponds to **Nicholas,** for it merely shortens the French **Nicolette.**

Colin (Cf. **Colan,** q.v.) Lit., 'a dove'. It derives from St Columba or Columbus. Scottish **Colin** is sometimes confused with Fr. **Colin,** which pet-forms **Nicolas.** Pet-name: **Col.**

Colman Likewise from L. columba, 'a dove'.

Columbine f. From It. **Colombina**, from the f. of L. columbinus, 'dove-like'.

Conal See **Connal**.

Conan m. This is a Breton, Irish, Welsh name.

Connaire The Gaelic form of Irish **Connor**, it means 'high will, high courage'.

Connal, Connel, Conal This Irish m. 'Christian' signifies, in Celtic, 'chief's, or high, courage'.

Connie Diminutive of **Constance**.

Connor See **Connaire**.

Conrad In Teutonic, originally **Kuonrat** (cf. the old Mercian king, **Cenred**), 'shrewd in advice'. A name famous in medieval European history.

Constance Less probably from L. constans (see **Constantine**, than from constantia (see **Constantia**), though admittedly constantia is, in L., a derivative of constans.

Constant m. An English and Irish shortening of **Constantine**, in common with which it is, in C20, becoming rare.

Constantia From L., it means 'constancy'.

Constantine m. From L. **Constantinus**, originally a diminutive of **Constantius**, itself from constans, 'constant, firm'. Its use in England results from the fame of Constantine the Great.

Cora This Irish and American name comes from Gr. koré, a maiden; its popularity in the U.S.A. may owe much to Byron's poem.

Coral f. From the prettiness of coral; cf. **Pearl**.

Coralie A derivative from the preceding.

Cordelia is a Celtic name, perhaps meaning 'daughter of the sea'.

Corinna From a Gr. f. Christian name, presumably a diminutive of koré (see **Cora**).

Cormac Lit., 'charioteer'. **Cormac** is a name prominent in Irish legend, in early Irish history, in the early Irish Church, and, since C7 as a 'Christian' throughout Ireland.

Cormick A variant of the preceding.

Cornelia f.; **Cornelius**, m. The **Corn**- may be L. cornu, a horn, the symbol of kingship; -elia, -elius is an adjectival suffix.

Corney An Irish pet-form, hence an independent variant, of the preceding.

Corrie Diminutive of **Cornelia(-ius), Cora, Cordelia, Cormick.**

Cosmo An Italian, thence English, contraction of It. **Cosimo,** at one time a very aristocratic name, meaning 'order': Gr. kosmos.

Courtenay, Courtney is properly a surname.

Cradock An English contraction of **Caradoc.**

Crispian, Crispin The former represents L. **Crispianus,** the latter **Crispinus:** 'two brothers who accompanied St Quentin when he preached the Gospel in France. They settled at Soissons, and there . . . supported themselves by making shoes until their martyrdom, A.D. 287'. (Yonge.)

Crystal See **Chrystal.**

Curtis m. An American 'Christian' from the surname, itself perhaps from Old Fr. (le) curteis, '(the) courteous (man)'.

Cuthbert A.-S. **Cuthbeorht,** lit. 'famous-bright', hence probably 'famous splendour'. Pet-forms: **Cuth** and, in Northern dialects, **Cuddy.**

Cynthia The goddess Artemis (Diana) was so called because she was born at Mt Cynthus in Delos, the smallest of the Cyclades in the Aegean Sea. Pet-form: **Cyn,** pronounced **Sin.**

Cyprian See **Ciprian.**

Cyril Gr. **Kurillos,** lit. 'lordly', from kurios, 'a lord or master'.

Cyrus In C19-20, much more common in America than in the Commonwealth, **Cyrus** (from the Gr. **Kuros**) owes its popularity to the founder of the Persian Empire. Pet-form: **Cy,** pronounced Si.

D

Daff, Daffy Diminutive of **Daphne.**

Dafod A Welsh form of **David.**

Dagmar Originally Danish, it represents 'Dane's joy'.

Dai A Welsh m. 'Christian', possibly—like Fr. De—from a **Celtic** word meaning 'fire'. (Celtic dei, to shine.)

Daisy is the flower, which is A.S. 'daeges eage, day's eye, from its opening in the morning and also from its appearance'. (Weekley.)

Daly See **Elaine.**

Damian Gr. **Damianos,** it signifies 'one who tames', from damáö, I tame. There are four Saints Damian. With the variant **Damien,** this name is now rare except among Catholics.

Dan Both a diminutive of **Daniel** and a m. 'Christian' in its own right. In Heb., **Daniel** means 'God is my judge'.

Dandie A Scottish m., it is a corruption of **Andrew.**

Daniel See **Dan.**

Daphne This f. name, deriving from the Gr., means a bay-tree.

Mythological Daphne, pursued by amorous Apollo, was by the gods transformed into this tree, henceforth Apollo's favourite.

Darby like **Dermot**, is the commonly employed English variant of the Irish **Diarmid** or **Diarmaid**, a freeman.

Darcy, D'Arcy This is the English form of the Irish **Dorchaida**, or of the patronymic **O'Dorchaidhe**. Often, however, it comes from the French surname **D'Arcy**, 'he of Arcy'.

Darius In Persian 'wealthy', this name is now comparatively rare even in the U.S.A.

Darrel(l); Daryl This attractive m. name means 'darling' and derives from an A.S. word.

David 'The man after God's own heart' was named from the Heb. verb 'to love'. Like **John**, it strikes very few people as being Hebraic. Diminutives: **Dave, Davie.**

Dawfydd The usual Welsh form of **David**. Cf. **Dafod.**

Dawn f., is the English answer to **L. Aurora.**

Day An Anglicization of **Dai**—except as a Cornish m. name, when it may represent (St) **Deicolus**, 'God-server'.

Deb, Debby The usual diminutives of:

Deborah In Heb., 'a bee'.

Deiniol The Welsh 'shape' or **Daniel.**

Deirdre (less often, **Derdre**) has, in C20, become fashionable among actresses, authoresses, and women artists. From Old Celtic **Derdriu**, 'The Raging One'.

Delia A 'surname' of Artemis, as **Delius** is of Apollo; from the Gr. island of Delos.

Delicia From It. delizia, 'delight'.

Della 'seems to be purely fanciful' (**Jack and Jill** perhaps a blend of **Delia+Bella**).

Demetrius m. Gr., 'of Demeter', originally 'vowed to Demeter', the goddess protecting the fruits of the earth.

Denis loosely **Dennis**. Adopted from Fr., but ultimately from **Dionysos**, the Gr. god of wine and revelry.

Denise properly a Fr. name, is the f. companion to **Denis**.

Denzil or, less correctly, **Densil**, is a mainly Cornish m. name, perhaps cognate with **Denis**.

Derek The most general C20 form of **Derrick**.

Dermot See **Diarmaid**.

Derrick is a Dutch pet-form of the name corresponding to **Theodoric**.

Desmond is an Irish clan-name become a surname, become a given name; literally 'South Munster'.

Detta Sometimes an English contraction of **Henrietta**, but at other times a shortening of It. Benedetta (cf. **Benedict**).

Dhugal m. A solely Celtic name; it means 'black, i.e. swarthy, stranger'. Also **Dougal**.

Di The diminutive of both **Dinah** and **Diana**.

Diamond f. A 'jewel-name': cf. **Beryl, Emerald, Pearl, Ruby**.

Diana was an ancient Italian divinity, whom the Romans identified with the Greek Artemis. At Rome, Diana was the goddess of light; she represented the moon.

Diarmaid, Diarmid A Celtic name, meaning 'a freeman', frequently heard in both Ireland and Scotland. It figures prominently in legend and in history. Anglicized as **Dermot**.

Dick A shortening of obsolete **Diccon**, an English transformation of **Richard**.

Digby is properly a surname.

Diggory m., is probably of Fr. origin.

Dinah Heb. 'judged'.

Dodo An English contraction of **Dorothea**.

Doll, Dolly An English contraction of **Dorothea**.

Dolly A pet-form, both of **Doll** and of **Adolphus**.

Dolores Originally and mainly Sp. ('sorrows': cf. Our Lady of Sorrows: **Maria de Dolores**), from L. dolor, 'grief'.

Dominic By way of Fr. **Dominique** from L. dominicus, it means 'child born on Sunday'.

Donald The English form of **Domhnall**, 'world-ruler'.

Donoghue Celtic, perhaps for 'brown chieftain'.

Dora Adapted from Ger. **Dore**, a contraction of **Dorothea**.

Dorcas Gr., 'gazelle'.

Doreen Although probably of Irish origin, it is usually a diminutive of **Dora**.

Dorinda A fancy embellishment, of **Dora, Dorothea, Dorothy**.

Doris Lit., 'a Doric girl'.

Dorothea In Gr., 'a gift (doron) of God (**Theos**)'. Of this widespread European name, the Ger. form is the same as the English, though the more English 'shape' is **Dorothy**.

Dot A diminutive of **Dorothea** and **Dorothy**. Avoid the diminutive **Dotty**.

Dougal See **Dhugal**.

Douglas Originally a Scottish name, meaning 'dark-stream'; from a clan-name, it became a surname, then a given name. Pet-forms: **Doug, Duggie**.

Dowal An Irish form of the Scottish **Dougal** and **Dugald**.

Dreda f. Probably a shortening of **Etheldreda**.

Drew m. Brought to England by a follower of William the Conqueror, this name derives from Old Fr., dru, sturdy.

Dudley Properly a surname.

Duff m. This Scottish name represents Celtic **Dhu**, lit. 'the black man', i.e. 'he of the swarthy countenance'.

Dugald In Celtic, lit. 'dark stranger'.

Duggie Diminutive of **Douglas** and **Dugald**.

Duke Both **Duke** and **Earl,** as given names, are rare in the Commonwealth, but common in the United States.

Dulcie, Dulcia From L. dulcis, sweet.

Duncan Of Celtic origin, this Scottish 'Christian' means 'brown warrior'.

Dunstan An A.S. name equivalent to 'hillstone', in reference to physical strength or moral firmness; cf. **Peter.**

Dylan is a Welsh m. name, lit., 'sea, ocean'.

E

Eachaid, Eachan m. Lit., in Celtic, 'a horse'.

Eamon The Irish for **Edmund.**

Earl or **Earle** See **Duke.**

Eb, Ebbie Diminutives of:

Ebenezer m. A Heb. word meaning 'stone of help'.

Ed Familiar pet-name for **Edgar, Edmund, Edward, Edwin.**

Eda Originally a diminutive of **Edith.**

Eddie A diminutive of **Edward, Edwin, Edmund.**

Edgar In A.-S., **Eadgar,** meaning 'prosperous spear'.

Edie The usual 'endearment' of:

Edith In A.S., **Eadgyth,** 'prosperous war'. As used by the Normans in England, it lumps together the A.S. names **Eadgyth, Eadgifu** ('rich gift'), **Eadgifa** ('giver of bliss'), and even **Aelfgifu** ('elf-gift').

Edmond, Edmund In A.S., **Eadmund** ('happy protection'); the -ond form is Gallic.

Edna A contraction of the long-obsolete **Edina,** itself probably the f. of **Edwin;** Heb., 'rejuvenation', (Webster.)

Edward In A.S. **Eadward,** 'rich guardian'. Charlotte Yonge hymns it as 'the most really noted of all our own genuine appellations. . . .'

Edwin In A.S. **Eadwine,** lit., 'rich friend'.

Effie A contraction and diminutive of **Euphemia,** but in C20 often bestowed independently.

Egbert In A.S., **Ecgbeorht,** literally 'edge-bright'.

Egmont It means 'sword protection'.

Eileen is a genuinely Celtic name: **Eilh(i)lin.** One of the numerous benefits conferred by the Irish literary revival of late C19-early C20.

Eiluned is a Welsh f. name.

Elaine A variant of **Ellen,** i.e. of **Helen.**

Eleanor, Eleanora, Eleanore English variants of **Helen;** directly, however, **Eleanor** and **Eleanore** derive from the Provençal **Aliénor.**

Eli has two independent existences. A diminutive of the next three names, it is also a Biblical name in its own right (see 1 Samuel, i. 9), with the literal meaning: 'high'.

Elias Heb 'God the Lord'; cf. the next.

Elijah Lit., in Heb., 'Jehovah is God'.

Elihu A Heb. name, meaning either 'God is Jehovah' (cf. **Elijah**) or perhaps 'God—or, the Lord—himself'.

Elinor A mere variant of **Eleanor.**

Eliot See **Elliot.**

Elisabeth See **Elizabeth.**

Elise Properly and mostly Fr., this is a variant of **Eliza.**

Elisha In C19-20 it occurs chiefly in the U.S.A., where most of the 'prophets' reside. Heb., 'God is salvation'.

Eliza was, originally, a contraction, introduced by the Elizabethan poets, of **Elizabeth;** now apprehended as an independent name. Pet-name: **Liza.**

Elizabeth, Elisabeth Heb., 'consecrated to God'. It is known in many forms: e.g., **Eliza, Bess, Bessy, Bet, Beth, Betsy, Betty, Liz, Lizzie, Liza, Lisa, Libby.** The original name was **Elisheba,** and this has developed, through Greek and Latin, into **Elisabeth,** whence **Elizabeth. Elizabeth** has long been famous in history both political and ecclesiastical.

Ella A variant of **Ellen.**

Ellen A Scottish (hence English) pronunciation of **Helen.**

Ellie. A diminutive of **Eleanor** and **Helena.**

Elliot, Elliott, Eliot A very English derivative of:

Ellis (For origin, see **Elias.**) In C18-20, it is mostly a surname, but, as a 'Christian', it has considerable merit.

Elma f. If Gr., it signifies 'love'; if A.S., 'like an elm'.

Elmer is merely an American metamorphosis of **Aylmer**.

Eloisa, Eloise These may be f. forms and derivatives of **Lewis (Louis)**; but the name more probably Gallicizes the Old German **Helewidis**.

Elsa, Else Originally Ger., it means 'noble maiden'.

Elsie Contraction of **Elizabeth**.

Elspeth, Elspie Scottish derivatives from **Elizabeth**.

Elvina like **Malvina**, is a Celtic f. name of romantic associations; lit., 'friendly'.

Elvira is a Sp. name of unknown origin.

Elza A rather affected form of **Elsa**.

Emanuel, Emmanuel Originally **Immanuel**, it derives from Heb., where it probably means 'God with us'.

Emerald A jewel-name.

Emery A variant of **Emmery**.

Emile Originally and mainly French, it derives from L. **Aemilius**, the name of an important Roman clan.

Emily From L. **Aemilia**; see **Emile**. Pet-form: **Em**.

Emlyn A Welsh m. name that perhaps derives from L. **Aemilianus**.

Emma, 'Emma comes, via Imma, from Irma, short for some such name as Ermintrude, in which the first element is the name of a Teutonic deity and the second as in Gertrude' (**Jack and Jill**). Often shortened to **Em**, pet-form: **Emmie**.

Emmanuel See **Emanuel**.

Emmelina, Emmeline Originally diminutives, now regarded as elaborations, of **Emilia** and **Emily**.

Emmery, Emery A pleasant Anglicization of **Almeric(k)**.

Emmie, Emmy Diminutive form of **Emma, Emily, Emmelina.**

Emott f. and, derivatively, m. A mainly North of England name, probably developed from **Em,** the original English form of **Emma.**

Emrys m. This Welsh name represents a drastic transformation of **Ambrose** or its L. predecessor **Ambrosius.**

Ena Perhaps a contraction of **Edana** (see **Edna**), or **Edina.**

Enid This is one of those names which would entail on its owner a very grave responsibility, if in the Celtic it means 'spotless purity', as some have held. In Arthurian romance, Enid was the metaphorical torch-bearer of virtuous and noble womanhood.

Enoch In Heb., 'dedication', hence 'dedicated' (to God).

Ephraim Heb., 'two-fold increase' or 'doubly fruitful'.

Eppie f. An English diminutive of **Euphemia.**

Erasmus From Gr. erao, 'I love'.

Eric Of old Norse origin; literally, perhaps 'ever king'. Pet-name **Rick.**

Erica The female form of the preceding.

Ermin m., comes from the name of a Teutonic demi-god.

Erminia The f. of the preceding.

Ermintrude (In Ger., **Irmentrud** or **-de**) See **Emma.**

Ernest From the Ger. **Ernst,** earlier **Ernust,** earnestness. Pet-forms: **Ern** and **Ernie.**

Ernestine A melodious f. derivative from the preceding.

Ernie See **Ernest.**

Errol m. Ultimately from the L. and signifying 'wandering' or 'wanderer' (Loughead).

Esau Heb. 'hairy'.

Esmé m. and f. 'Apparently the past participle of O.Fr. esmer, to esteem' (Weekley) ; hence, like **Amabel,** from the L. amare, 'to love'.

Esmeralda Mostly a Sp. name, it is, lit., 'an emerald'.

Esmond 'Desmond, Esmond and Redmond were taken to Ireland by the Vikings' (**Jack and Jill**). Teutonic, **Esmond** perhaps means 'divine protection'. Pet-form : **Es.**

Essie A diminutive of **Esther,** but occasionally used as a self-contained name independent of any reference thereto.

Estelle A diminutive of :

Esther From Persian satarah or Assyrian sitarch (perhaps, as Weekley suggests, from the Persian for 'the planet Venus'), through Gr. aster, 'a star', which in the Septuagint becomes, as a name, **Hesther.**

Ethel In A.S., **Aethelu,** 'noble', never stood alone as a f. name ; usually it preceded a noun, the pair forming such names as **Ethelgiva,** 'noble gift'. Pet-name : **Eth.**

Ethelbert In A.S., 'noble splendour'.

Ethelburga Lit., 'noble protectress'.

Etheldred (now rare), **Etheldreda** (not quite so rare). See **Audrey.**

Ethelred, Ethered 'Aethlred, Noble-speech or counsel, the brother of Alfred, was almost canonized by his subjects, and is sometimes called Ethered, whence the Scottish Ethert, (Yonge).

Etta A shortening of **Henrietta;** a diminutive of **Esther.**

Ettie, Etty A diminutive of **Esther.**

Eugene m. In Gr., 'well-born', this is one of a group of names beginning with eu, 'well' or 'happily'. The Gr. **Eugeneios** became the Latin **Eugenius,** the Fr. **Eugène** and the German **Eugen.**

Eunice It derives from the Gr. eunis, 'a wife'.

Euphemia In Gr., the word means 'fair speech'. Pet-form : **Effie.**

Eustace m. This Gr. name probably means 'rich in ears of corn', i.e., 'happy in harvest'. Pet-forms : **Eus** and **Stace**.

Eva, Eve The former was adopted from Medieval Latin, the latter from Medieval French; themselves from Heb. **Hawwah**, lit. 'life' or 'living'—therefore cf. **Zoe**.

Evadne f. In Gr., her name was **Euädne, ?** 'the well-tamed'.

Evan like **Ewan** or **Ewen**, represents the Celtic **Eoghan**, 'young warrior'. But **Evan** is also the Welsh form of **John**.

Evangeline Lit., 'happy messenger'.

Eve See **Eva**.

Eveleen In Celtic, 'pleasant', this is the original and in Ireland the commonest form of **Eveline**. Ultimately, the name may go back to the Heb. word for 'life'.

Evelina An ornamental variant of :

Eveline (For origin, see **Eveleen**). This, not **Evelyn**, is the truly English feminine form.

Evelyn Originally m., perhaps from the Celtic for 'pleasant', it has, in C19-20, been used for both sexes; for the f., both **Eveleen** and **Eveline** are preferable, except when **Evelyn** is meant to represent the surname **Evelyn**. Female pet-name: **Evvie**.

Everard or **Everett** Lit., 'Strong or courageous as a wild boar'.

Ewan or **Ewen** See **Evan**.

Ewart An English contraction of **Everard**.

Ezekiel Since, in Heb., it signifies 'God will strengthen', it should be compared with **Hezekiah**, 'strength of the Lord'. Pet-name: **Zeke**.

Ezra Heb. for 'help'. It was Ezra who, ca. 536 B.C., led the Jews back from the Babylonian captivity. Pet names : **Ez**.

F

Fabian m. Lit., 'bean-grower', from L. faba, a bean.

Faith (Cf. **Charity** and **Hope.**) This Scriptural-virtue f. name appealed to the Puritans, survives in rural districts, and is still fairly common among Nonconformists.

Fanny is strictly a pet-form of **Frances,** but it has long been treated as wholly independent.

Fay f. A variant of **Faith,** it is a revival of archaic fay, as in by my fay.

Felicia A variant of :

Felicity A natural English adaption of Fr. **Félicité, Felicity** comes from L. felicitas, 'happiness', itself from felix, 'happy'.

Felix Direct from L., felix, 'happy'. Common to Britain, France, Spain and Russia, it is a name particularly significant in the annals of the Church.

Fenella See **Finella.**

Ferdie A diminutive of :

Ferdinand From a Teutonic compound signifying 'venturous journey' or 'adventuring life', perhaps equivalent to 'one who leads an adventurous life', a knight errant.

Fergus A Celtic—mainly Irish and Scottish—m. 'Christian', it derives from a Celtic word meaning 'excellent choice'.

Finella, Fenella In Celtic, 'she of white shoulders'.

Fingal In Celtic, it is 'fair stranger' ; contrast **Dugald,** 'dark stranger' : both were originally epithets of racial designation, **Fingal** for a Norseman, **Dugald** for a Dane.

Fiona Lit., 'white (girl)' : from Gaelic fionn.

Fleur is the Fr., **Flower** the English, form of this flower-name par excellence.

Flora This f. name owes its popularity to **Flora** (L. flos, a flower), the Roman goddess of flowers and spring.

Florence f., comes from L. **Florentia**, from florens, 'flourishing'. It owes much of its popularity to Florence Nightingale. Pet-names: **Flo** and:

Florrie, Flossie Diminutives of **Flora** and **Florence**.

Flower See **Fleur**.

Frances f.,; **Francis** m. 'Mary Tudor, . . . in memory of her brief queenship of France', or as a compliment to King Francis of France 'christened her first child Frances—that Lady Frances Brendon . . ., who had numerous namesakes among the maidens of the Tudor court. The masculine came in at the same time, and burst into eminence in the Elizabethan cluster of worthies—Drake, Walsingham, Bacon' (Yonge). **Francis** derives from Old Ger. **Franco**, 'a free lord'. **Frances** has pet-name **Fran**.

Francesca This is the Italian form of **Frances**.

Francis See **Frances**.

Frank The more English form of **Francis**.

Frankie A pet-name for **Frances, Francis, Frank.**

Franklin properly a surname (lit., 'freeholder'), has, in the U.S.A., been often bestowed as a 'Christian'; since ca. 1785, in honour of Benjamin Franklin, statesman, scientist, writer; a popularity increased by the fame of that even greater man, Franklin Delano Roosevelt.

Fred, Freddie, Freddy Pet-names for **Frederic.**

Freda A pet-form of **Winifred** rather than an Anglicized variant of **Frida.**

Frederica A Portuguese and English f. of **Frederic(k).**

Frederic or **Frederick** occasionally **Fredric** In Fr., **Frédéric**, in Ger., **Friedrich** (whence **Fritz**) ; lit., 'peace-rule', hence 'peaceful ruler'.

Frida more generally **Frieda** A Ger. f. name (lit., 'peace') that has gained some hold in England. Diminutive: Free.

Fritz An occasional diminutive of **Frederic(k)**, it is properly the pet-form of the Ger. equivalent **Fri(e)drich**.

Fulbert A long-established English m. 'Christian', it derives from Teutonic, where it means 'exceeding bright'.

Fulk or **Fulke** is a fine old m. name, but properly a surname. From Old Ger. **Fulco**, 'one of the folc or people'.

G

Gabriel In Heb., it means 'man of God'.

Gabriella, Gabrielle f. Etymology as for **Gabriel, Gabriella** is primarily It. and Sp., as **Gabrielle** is primarily Fr.: English hospitality has done the rest.

Gail This diminutive of **Abigail** is sometimes bestowed as an independent f.

Garnet As m., probably 'little Warren': Anglo-Norman **Guarin**+ the diminutive suffix -**et**. As a f., it is of different origin: straight from garnet—cf. **Amber, Pearl, Ruby.** (Withycombe.)

Garret, Garrett A variant of the rare **Garth**.

Garrie, Garry The diminutive of **Garret** and **Garth,** but now sometimes bestowed independently.

Garth m. This is a modern form of **Gareth,** knightly as In Tennyson's Idyll, **Gareth and Lynette,** 1872. The A.S. is **Garrath,** 'firm spear'.

Gary m. This predominantly American name probably derives from the surname, with some influence from **Garrie,** q.v.

Gaston m. Properly and mostly Fr.

Gatty f. A characteristically English contraction of **Gertrude.**

Gavin A mainly Scottish name (m.), **Gavin** in its Celtic original perhaps means 'hawk (gwalch) of the month of May'.

Gawain, Gawaine now usually **Gawen.** This is the English equivalent of the Scottish **Gavin** and was popular in the Middle Ages.

Gay A woman's name, direct from the adjective.

Gene The usual diminutive of **Eugene** and **Eugenia.**

Genevieve Perhaps 'fair girl', it comes from Celtic.

Genevra An English contraction of **Guinevere.**

Geoffrey occasionally **Geoffroy** Gallicized forms of **Godfrey** or rather of its Teutonic original **(Gottfrid, Gottfried),** meaning 'God's peace'. Pet-name: **Geoff.** See also **Jeffery.**

Geordie A Scottish and North Country variant of:

George comes from Gr. georgos, 'an earth-worker', i.e. 'a husbandman'. The usual early 'Christian' was **Georgios** or -**ius** and it became general through the fame of St George, Patron of England.

Georgiana, Georgina f. derivatives of **George.**

Georgie, Georgy A diminutive of **George, Georgiana, Georgina.** Also it is the f. form of **George.**

Gerald comes from Old Fr. **Giralt,** itself related to Old Ger. **Gerwald,** 'spear-wielder'.

Geraldine The English f. of Gerald.

Gerard Lit., 'spear-hard'—formidable with the spear.

Gert, Gertie Diminutives of the next; **Gert** is thought rather vulgar.

Gertrude Ger. **Gertrud,** Old Ger. **Gertrut,** 'beloved spear'.

Gervas (rare), **Gervase** or **Gervaise** Of unknown origin; perhaps Teutonic and meaning 'spear-servant'.

Gibbon is an English transformation of **Gilbert.**

Gideon In Heb., 'a destroyer', a great soldier.

Gil A pet-form of the next two names.

Gilbert In Old Ger., **Gisilbert, Giselbert, Gislebert,** 'bright pledge'; whence, by contraction, **Gilbert.**

Gilchrist In Celtic, 'servant of Christ'.

Giles This English and Scottish name, popular enough at one time to have become a surname, is of doubtful origin.

Gill A shortening of **Gillian.**

Gillespie m. and f. Properly a Scottish name, derived from the Celtic for 'the servant of a bishop'.

Gillian f., is 'the popular form of **Juliana,** which, for some unknown reason, was a favourite medieval font-name'. (Weekley).

Gillie A diminutive of **Gilbert.**

Gillies m. In Celtic, it represents 'servant of Jesus'.

Gilmour m. This Scottish 'Christian' is lit., in Celtic, 'servant of Mary'. For others of the religious 'servant' group, see **Gilchrist, Giles** (perhaps), **Gillespie,** and **Gillies.**

Gip A pet-form of **Gilbert.**

Girzie A Scottish diminutive of **Griseldis, Grizel.**

Gladys The Welsh form of **Claudia.**

Gloria pet-form, **Glory**. From L. gloria, fame.

Goddard In Ger., **Gotthard,** from Old Ger. **Godehard,** this English m. font-name means 'God-strong; hence, pious'.

Godfrey From Teutonic, it denotes 'God's peace'.

Godwin Teutonic for 'God-friend', i.e. excellent friend.

Gordon m. From the Scottish surname, it owes something to the fame of General Gordon († 1885).

Goronwy A Welsh m., of obscure origin.

Grace Cf. those other theological abstractions: **Faith, Hope, Charity, Mercy,** and **Prudence.** It means, in Latin, 'thanks' or 'gratitude', 'favour' or 'bounty'. Diminutive: **Gracie.**

Graham is properly a surname.

Graine, Grainne, Graina f. An Irish 'Christian', it represents, in Celtic, 'love'.

Grant Strictly, a surname. Mostly American.

Gray or **Grey** Strictly a surname.

Greg (Northern) and **Grig** (Southern). These are diminutives of **Gregory**; but also an independent Scottish m. name, meaning 'fierce', with variant **Greig.**

Gregory This m. 'Christian' is as delightful as it is dignified: it is, in itself, euphonious without being luxurious, clangorous without harshness; and it has a brilliant ecclesiastical representation. Lit., 'a watchman'; shorter form, **Gregor,** mostly Scottish.

Greta Either an Englishing of **Grete,** a Ger. contraction of **Margaret,** or, more probably, an adoption of the Swedish **Greta,** likewise a contraction.

Griffin See:

Griffith An English and Welsh m. name, the Welsh original being **Gruffydd.** The Welsh merely adapted **Rufus,** 'red (-haired)' or 'ruddy (-cheeked)', and in the same way turned the derivative **Rufinus** into **Gruffyn**, i.e. **Griffin**.

Griselda The English form of the mainly Scottish:

Griseldis In Teutonic, 'grey battle-maid'.

Grisell, Grissel, Grissil. Variants of **Grizel.**

Grizel, Grizell or **Grizzell; Grizzie** Scottish contractions of **Griseldis.**

Gruffydd The Welsh original of **Griffith.**

Guendolen diminutive **Guen.** See **Gwendolen.**

Guenever' Guenevere See **Guinevere.**

Guido An Italian 'shape' of **Guy.**

Guinevere, Guenevere Celtic, this name has a first element. (guen, gwen) that means 'white' (cf. **Gwendolen**); and the entire name appears to mean 'white wave'.

Gus The usual diminutive of **Augustus.** Contrast: **Gussie** (or -sy). Pet-form of **Augustus.**

Gustavus This English name is dying out, despite its rich historical associations. In Teutonic, it signifies either 'the divine staff' or 'the staff of the Goths' (cf. pillar of the Church).

Guy Perhaps from Celtic ('sense'), more probably from Old Ger. **Wido** of obscure meaning (? 'leader').

Gwalchmai A Welsh form of **Gavin.**

Gwen, Gwenda Diminutives of **Gwendolen.**

Gwendolen (or -in or -ine), this is the modern form of a Celtic name doubleted with **Guinevere** (earlier **Gwenever**); often spelt **Guendolen.** The first element means 'white'.

Gwenfrewi A Welsh form of **Winifred.**

Gwenhwyfar A Welsh variation of **Guinevere.**

Gwennie, Gwenny A diminutive of **Gwendolen.**

Gwenwynwyn, m. From the Celtic and perhaps meaning 'thrice-white' or 'thrice-fair'.

Gwilym is the Welsh form of **William.**

Gwladys A Welsh form of **Claudia.**

Gwyneth A mainly Welsh f., meaning 'blessed'.

Gwynne' f. In Celtic, 'white'.

H

Haidée A Fr. f. that has, since ca. 1930, become fairly general on the stage; often Anglicized as **Haidee** and pronounced **Háydee.** From the Gr., it should mean 'modest'.

Hal rarely **Hall.** A diminutive, much less common than it used to be, of **Henry** or, rather, of **Harry.**

Haldane m. Lit., 'half-Dane', it derives from Teutonic.

Hallam Properly a surname.

Hamilton Properly a surname. Pet-form: **Ham.**

Hamish This is the Gaelic form of **James.**

Hank An American diminutive of **Henry,** it comes immediately from Ger. **Hanke** (for **Heinrich**).

Hannah A doublet of **Anne.**

Hannibal Phoenician, 'grace of Baal'. Hannibal was that

Carthaginian general (246-182 B.C.) who defeated the Romans at Cannae, only to be himself defeated by Scipio, fourteen years later (202 B.C.).

Hanno This mainly Cornish m. name is from the Phoenician word that forms the first element of **Hannibal.**

Harding An English m. 'Christian' from Teutonic **Hardwin,** it means, lit., 'firm friend'.

Harold In Danish and Norwegian **Harald,** and **Harivald** in Old Norse, it is a compound denoting 'army-wielder', hence perhaps 'powerful general'.

Harriet occasionally **Harriot.** In Teutonic, 'home-rule'; the f. of **Harry;** probably influenced by Fr. **Henriette,** the f. of **Henri.**

Harry sometimes bestowed as an independent font-name, is a very old pet-name for **Henry;** its great popularity dates from the exploits of Henry V (1387-1422).

Hartley seems to have derived from the surname ('hard lea', perhaps 'stony meadow').

Harty An English variation of **Hester** and **Harriet.**

Harvey From Fr. **Hervé,** from the heroic Ger. **Herewig,** 'warrior-war', i.e. '(land-) war warrior'.

Hatty An English transformation of **Harriet.**

Hazel f. From the tree and nut so named.

Heather f. From the shrub.

Hebe f. To be avoided, for it is now generic for a barmaid. In any event, dissyllabic.

Hector Gr., 'defender'; from that Hector who was the chief hero of the Trojans in their war with the Greeks some 3,000 years ago.

Hedley Strictly a surname.

Helen, Helena The former is an English and Scottish shortening of the latter, which is very rare in Scotland. **Helena,** found also in Sp. and Portuguese, Ger. and Dutch, represents the Gr. **Helené** ('Ελένη), the f. of **Helenos,** lit., 'the bright' or 'the light' from a word signifying heat or light: cf. **Helios,** the sun-god.

Heloïsa f. A blend of Fr. **Héloïse** and It. **Eloïsa.**

Henrietta The f. of **Henry;** cf. **Harriet.**

Henry Old Ger. **Heimirich'** modern **Heinrich,** lit., 'ruler of an enclosure'; via Fr. **Henri.**

Hephzibah A Biblical name: Heb., 'My delight is in her'.

Herbert In Teutonic, it means 'bright army', hence 'glorious warrior'. A Norman brought it to England ca. 1070. Pet-form: **Herb** or **Herbie.**

Hercules m. Now rare, it honours the Classical equivalent of Samson. The Gr. **Herakles,** 'lordly fame'.

Hermione Gr., 'daughter of Hermes'. In Shakespeare's 'A Winter's Tale', she is the loved and much-wronged wife of Leontes.

Hero In Gr., 'a lady' or 'mistress of the house'.

Hesketh is properly a surname.

Hester A variant of **Esther.**

Hetty A diminutive of **Esther (Hester)** and **Henrietta.**

Hew, Hu An English and, more particularly, Welsh m. 'Christian' from a Celtic word signifying 'mind'.

Hezekiah See **Ezekiel** for the origin.

Hi Short for **Hiram.**

Hilaria f. A derivative of:

Hilary m. and occasionally f. By way of **Hilarius** from L. hilaris, 'cheerful'.

Hilda Chief among the Valkyries was **Hild (Hildr, Hildur,** or **Hiltia).** In Teutonic the word means 'battle' and has thus come to mean battle-maid.

Hildebrand m. From Old German for 'battle sword'.

Hildegard or **-garde** f. Another name from Old Ger.: lit., 'battle-wand', hence 'battle maiden'.

Hiram m., is rare in England. It is related to the old-fashioned **Hierom,** which led to **Jerome;** Heb., 'most noble'.

Hobart An English variant of **Hubert.**

Hoel or **Howell** This Welsh m. 'anglicizes' Welsh hywel, 'lordly'.

Homer implies a compliment to one of the world's three or four greatest poets. The Gr. **Homeros** personifies a Gr. word meaning 'pledge' or 'hostage'.

Honor f. Direct from the L. for 'honour'.

Honora, Honoria From the preceding.

Hope f. Originally Puritan, it is of the same class as **Honor, Faith. Charity, Mercy** and **Patience.**

Horace The Horatian gens or clan, very old and noble, was memorable for the battle of the Horatii, in the mythical times of early Rome. Diminutive: **Horrie.**

Horatia The f. of:

Horatio A variant of **Horace,** probably suggested by It. **Orazio.** Its C19-20 use is mainly prompted by hero-worship for Horatio Nelson.

Hortensia The f. of the obsolete **Hortensius,** 'a gardener'.

Hosea represents, in Heb., 'salvation'.

Howard From the surname, which, like **Percy** and **Stanley,** is very aristocratic in its connexions. It has various origins.

Howell See **Hoel.**

Hu A variant of **Hew.**

Hubert m., is, in Teutonic, 'mind-bright'.

Hugh Perhaps—via. Fr.—a Germanic word meaning 'mind, thought'. It has long been a famous name in both Church and State.

Hugo Originally the L., then, much later, the Ger. form, of **Hugh;** hence an English one.

Hulda f. Mostly in U.S.A.; from Norwegian **Huldr,** lit. 'muffled'. But **Huldah** is Heb.: 'a weasel'.

Humbert m. A Teutonic name signifying 'bright giant'.

Humfrey or **Humfry** usually and barbarously, **Humphrey.** An alteration (after such Fr. names as **Geoffrey**) of A.S. **Hunfrith,** perhaps '(something) peace'.

I

Ian, Iain This Scottish m. is a variant of **John;** and **Iain** is the more Gaelic form (cf. Erse **Eoin**).

Ianthe f. Gr., perhaps 'violet flower'.

Ida Short for **Idonia,** once a common name.

Idris is a Welsh m., frequently bestowed.

Ifor The Welsh form of **Ivor.**

Ignatius comes, via L., from Gr. **Ignatios,** itself of unknown origin. Mostly a Catholic name.

Ike See **Isaac.**

Imogen, Imogine This old English f. name owes much to the charm of Shakespeare's Imogen in **Cymbeline.**

Ines, Inez These forms approximate to Sp. **Iñez,** which corresponds to English **Agnes.**

Ingram m. In Teutonic, either 'Ing's raven' or '(an) Angle's raven'.

Ingrid This pleasant f. name is Norwegian.

Innocent From L. innocens, 'harmless', later 'innocent'. Since it has provided the name of thirteen popes and one anti-pope, it is a mainly Catholic name.

Iolanthe; (obsolescent) **Yolande** f. Probably from Old Fr. **Violante,** which is perhaps connected with **Viola.**

Iolo is a Welsh name, probably for **Julius.**

Ira m. Mostly American; Heb. for 'watchful' or 'a watcher'.

Irene is from **Eirene,** the Gr. goddess of peace; the name is trisyllabic, with the stress on the second syllable.

Iris f., comes straight from the Gr. for a rainbow.

Irma f. See **Emma.**

Irving is strictly a surname.

Isaac in Heb., signifies 'laughter'. Pet-names: **Ike, Ikey.**

Isabel, Isobel Originally a transformation of **Elisabeth.** But it has also an independent origin as a Biblical name (1 Kings, xvi, 31).

Isabella An elaboration of the preceding.

Isadora f. Originally and mainly Sp., it would seem to form the f. of **Isidor(e),** from Gr. **Isidoros,** perhaps 'equal gift'. Pet-form: **Issy** or **Izzy.**

Iseult The same as **Ysolt,** but directly from Fr.

Ishmael m. Heb., 'God hearkens'.

Isidor, Isidore m. **Isidor** is mostly the Teutonic, **Isidore** the Fr., m. form of a name that Ernest Weekley brilliantly conjectured to signify 'gift of Isis'.

Isobel, Isobella See **Isabel** and **Isabella**.

Isold, Isolda, Isolde Romance forms of **Ysolt**.

Israel Heb., 'contending with the Lord'.

Ivan The Russian form of **John**.

Ivo In origin, this m. is the Breton name Yves, itself 'the Old French nominative of **Yvain,** identical with Evan and John' **(Jack and Jill)**.

Ivor Either an Irish, Scottish, and (as **Ifor**) Welsh form of the Viking name, **Ingwar,** ? 'protector of Ing', or, more probably, of Celtic origin—of the preceding entry.

Ivy f. A plant-name.

Izzy The diminutive of **Isidor, Ishmael, Isaac, Israel.**

J

Jabez m. Heb., 'height'; hence, 'tall one'.

Jack the usual pet-form of **John,** is sometimes bestowed independently. In America, the derivative **Jackson** (Jack's son) is not only a surname but, thanks to the fame of General Andrew Jackson (1767-1845), the seventh President of the U.S.A., and of General Thomas Jackson (1824-63), better known as 'Stonewall' Jackson, a not infrequent given-name.

Jacob Heb., 'a supplanter'. Pet-name: **Jake**; but also **Jack**. Akin to **James**.

Jacobina f. A counterpart of **Jacob**.

Jacqueline a Fr. f. derivative of **Jacques**.

Jago rare outside Cornwall, is an adoption of the Sp. form of **Jacob**.

Jake See **Jacob**.

James The Gr. **Iakobos** became L. **Jacobus,** whence French **Jacques,** whence 'in a way puzzling to phoneticians' Sp. **Jayme,** later **Jaime** (pronounced Hah-ee-may), whence, with the L. and Fr. ending is -s, our **James**. In Gaelic, James became **Hamish**; Ireland spells it **Seumas** (Shamus). Usual diminutive: **Jim**. Cockney **Jem**.

Jamesina The f.—mainly Scottish—of the preceding.

Jan A Welsh form of **John**; a shortening of **Janet**; a variant of:

Jane. An English contraction and transformation of **Joanna**. Diminutives: **Janey** and **Jenny, Jen**.

Janet A Scottish **Jane,** of which it was originally a diminutive.

Jarvis An English alteration of **Gervas**.

Jasmine Another flower-name for the use of girls. Variant: **Jessamine** (diminutive: **Jess**).

Jasper m. In Persian, 'master of the treasure'.

Jay originally a nickname (from the discordant bird) and then a surname, has in America become a Christian name.

Jean f. A Scottish variant of **Jane** and **Joan**. Diminutive: **Jeanie**.

Jedediah Heb., 'God is my friend'; diminutive, **Jed**.

Jeff A diminutive of **Jeffery** or **Jeffrey**.

Jefferson strictly a surname, has, in the U.S.A., been frequently bestowed as a 'Christian', commemorative of Thomas Jefferson (1743-1826), third President, and a great, practical-idealistic statesman.

Jeffery, Jeffrey An English variant of **Geoffrey.**

Jem, Jemmie, Jemmy Diminutives of **James.**

Jemima, Jemimah In Arabic, 'a dove'; in Heb., 'handsome as the day'. Diminutive: **Mima.**

Jen See **Jane.**

Jenkin A Welsh name and English diminutive of **(Jan** or) **John.**

Jennifer A delightful English adaptation of the Celtic **Winifred** or **Winifrid.**

Jenny An English contraction of **Johanna** and **Jane,** but now usually bestowed without reference to its original.

Jeremiah in Heb., means 'Jehovah has appointed'. The truly English form of the word is **Jeremy.**

Jeremy See **Jeremiah.**

Jermyn This ancient English m. derives from Fr. **Germain,** L. **Germanus,** a German.

Jerome Gr., 'holy name'. Sometimes **Jerram.**

Jerry The diminutive of **Jeremiah** (or -**ias**) and, occasionally, of **Jeremy** and **Jerome** and, loosely, of **Gerald.**

Jervis A modernization of **Gervas.**

Jess f. The pet-form of **Jessamine, Jessica** and **Jessie.**

Jessamine See **Jasmine.**

Jesse m. Heb., 'the Lord is'.

Jessica Heb. for 'God is looking'.

Jessie Properly, a pet-form either of **Jessica** or of **Janet.**

Jill The more usual form of **Gill,** the shortening of **Gillian.**

Jim, Jimmie, Jimmy Pet-forms of **James.**

Jinny A diminutive of **Jane.** Cf. **Jenny.**

Jo The pet-form of **Josephine** and **Joanna**; and, loosely, a variant of **Joe.**

Joachim An English contraction of the Heb. **Jehoiachim** or **Jehoiakim**, '(the) appointed of the Lord'.

Joan A contraction of **Johanna.**

Joanna See **Johanna.**

Job In Heb., 'persecuted' or 'afflicted'.

Jocelin m. L. jocus (cf. our jocose), 'merry', 'sportive'.

Jocelyn A variant of **Jocelin.**

Jock The Scottish pet-form of **John.**

Joe, Joey Diminutives of **Joseph.**

Joel m. Heb., 'Jehovah is God'.

Johanna, Joanna the more usual, although a 'derivative' of the other. Heb., 'God is gracious'.

John (See also **Jack.**) This name owes most of its vast European popularity to the Evangelist; its brevity and strength have contributed to make it, in the minds of the majority, the finest of all m. 'Christians'. From Heb.: 'God is gracious'.

Johnnie, Johnny A diminutive of **John.**

Jonah m. Heb., 'a dove'.

Jonas A Greco-Latin form of the preceding.

Jonathan Heb., 'the Lord's gift'.

Jordan Heb., 'descender' (lit., 'going down').

Joseph Heb., 'he shall add', 'increaser', 'addition'. It is interesting to learn that whereas there are some eighty-four Saints John, there are only fourteen canonized Josephs.

Josepha The f. properly of L. **Josephus**, hence of **Joseph**.

Josephine A f. diminutive of **Joseph**.

Josh A diminutive of:

Joshua Heb., 'the Lord (is my) salvation', a fitting name for him who led the Israelites to the Promised Land.

Josiah Heb., 'Jehovah supports'.

Josie A diminutive of **Josephine**.

Joy f. An 'abstract-virtue' name: cf. **Mercy, Hope, Honor.**

Joyce m. and f. It derives 'from Old Ger. **Gozo**, from **Gauta**, the root of the folk-name **Goth**. (Withycombe.)

Jude m. A contraction of the obsolete **Judah** and its variant **Judas**, it derives from Heb. 'praised' or 'praise' or 'praise of the Lord'.

Judith f., originally **Jehudith**, is a racial name: 'a Jewess'.

Judy Properly a diminutive of **Judith**, but occasionally employed as an independent font-name.

Jule The pet-form of the next six names.

Julia The f. of **Julius**.

Julian L. **Julianus**, a derivative of **Julius**.

Juliana The f. of the preceding.

Julie A softened form of **Julia**.

Juliet, Juliette From It. **Giulietta**, the diminutive of **Giulia**, itself from L. **Julia**.

Julius of obscure origin, has had a certain and enduring fame in the person of Julius Caesar. Diminutive: **Jule.**

June f. This attractive name was rare before C20.

Justin From L. **Justinus**, a m. diminutive of justus, 'just'.

K

Karen f. The Danish form of **Katharine** or **Katherine**.

Kate A diminutive, sometimes bestowed as an independent font-name, of the next three.

Katharina A variant of:

Katharine The name is perhaps a diminutive formed from Gr. kathara (the f.), 'pure', 'clean', 'unsullied'; and **Katharina (Catharina)** may have been the earlier shape of the word. But probably **Katharine** has—after Gr. **Katharas, -ra**—been folk-etymologized from Gr. **Aikaterinë,** a name of obscure origin. (Withycombe.)

Katherine A variant of the preceding.

Kath, Kathie Diminutives of **Katharine** and **Kathleen.**

Kathleen or **Cathleen** The Irish form of **Katherine.**

Katie, Katy A diminutive of **Katherine.**

Katrine An English shortening of **Katharine.**

Kay m. and f. As m., it represents the L. **Caius.** As f., it may have been suggested by **Katie**; more probably, however, it forms, originally, a diminutive of **Karen.**

Kean m. From Celtic cian, 'vast'.

Keith m., was originally the surname of a Scottish line of earls. In Gaelic, it means 'the wind'.

Kenelm m. Of A.S. origin, it signifies 'bold helmet'.

Kenneth Deriving from Celtic, it means 'handsome'. Pet-name: **Ken,** whence the diminutive **Kenny** or **Kennie.**

Kentigern m. A Welsh name, meaning 'head chief'.

Keren f., derives from Heb. **Kerenhappuch,** 'horn of eyelash-paint', the name of one of Job's daughters.

Kevin An Irish elaboration of **Kenneth.**

Keziah f. In Heb., 'cassia'.

Kieren or **Kieron** In Celtic, 'black'.

Kirstin f. A Scottish reduction of **Christian.**

Kirsty f. Scottish reduction of **Christian** and **Christine.**

Kit As a diminutive of **Christopher,** it is older than **Chris.** Moreover, it forms a variant of:

Kitty A diminutive of **Katharine.**

L

Lachlan m. From Old Norse, perhaps 'fjordland'.

Lalage In Greek, 'Prattler'.

Lambert Old Ger. **Landberht,** 'land-bright'.

Lance A diminutive of, or a substitute for:

Lancelot occ. **Lancilot;** anciently **Launcelot,** with **Launce** as a diminutive. Of fiercely disputed origin, **Launcelot** owes its currency to the most famous of King Arthur's Knights of the Round Table.

Lanty, Larry Irish diminutives of **Laurence** or **Lawrence.**

Laura would appear to have been coined from L. laurus, the laurel-tree, as a f. of **Laurence.** Diminutive: **Lolly.**

Laurence occasionally **Lawrence.** From L. **Laurentius** ('boy of the city of Laurentium'), probably from laurus, 'the laurel'.

Laurie The usual diminutive of **Laurence.**

Lavinia means 'a woman of Lavinium', a city in Italy.

Lawrence See **Laurence** Diminutive: **Lawrie.**

Lazarus m., is the Latin shape of the Greek **Lazaros**, representing Heb. **Eleazar,** 'whom God assists'.

Leah Heb., 'wearied'.

Leander Gr. 'lion-man'.

Leigh occasionally **Lee.** As a British m., it derives from the surname (lea, 'a meadow') ; as an American m., it usually commemorates the famous Southern general, Robert E. Lee (1807-70). As f., it derives from **Letitia.**

Leila occasionally **Leilah.** Probably from Arabic ('darkness'). Often Anglicized to **Lila.**

Lemuel m. Heb., 'devoted to God'.

Len A pet-form of **Leonard.** Diminutive: **Lennie** or **Lenny.**

Lena A reduction of **Eleanora** and **Leonora,** and a shortening of **Helena;** of. **Lina.** Occasionally, however, an adaption of Ger. **Lena,** itself for **Helen.**

Leo L (from Gr. leon), 'a lion'.

Leon m. From Gr. (see **Leo**), it is an Italian and Russian name that has made its way among English-speaking Jews.

Leonard 'Lion-hard', i.e. 'lion-strong', it is a hybrid from Gr. and Teutonic.

Leonie adapts the Fr. **Léonie,** f. of **Léon** (see **Leon**).

Leonora An abbreviation of Ger. **Eleanora.**

Leopold Via Fr. **Léopold,** from Old Ger. **Leutbald,** 'people-bold'.

Leot A Scottish transformation of **Loise.**

Lesbia comes straight from Latin: literally, 'girl of Lesbos'.

Leslie Properly a surname. Occasionally spelt **Lesley** and bestowed on girls. Pet-name: **Les.**

Lester From the surname **Lester,** i.e. 'he of Leicester'.

Letitia From L. laetitia, 'gladness'. Cf.:

Lettice An English 'shape' of It. **Letizia** (L. laetitia).

Letty A diminutive of **Letitia** and **Lettice.**

Levi Heb., 'joined'.

Lew The diminutive of **Lewis,** as **Lou** is of **Louis.**

Lewis has a double origin, for on the one hand it adapts the Welsh **Llewellyn** and therefore denotes 'lion-like', and on the other it anglicizes Fr. **Louis,** which, in its earliest form **Hhludowig** or **Hhlodowig,** denotes, in Teutonic, 'famous war'.

Liam m. An Irish name (**William**).

Libby A typically English derivation from **Elizabeth.**

Lida f. Originally Slavonic, it means 'people's love'.

Liddy The diminutive of **Lydia.**

Lil The diminutive of all **Lil-** names.

Lilias A popular Scottish form of:

Lilian, Lillian Of obscure origin, this f. name has been influenced by L. lilium (plural lilia), a lily.

Lilith f., means, in Heb., either serpent or vampire.

Lily occasionally **Lilly.** Probably a shortening (**Lili**) of **Lilian;** perhaps direct from English lily. Pet-name: **Lil.**

Lin A diminutive of **Lionel** and **Lindsay, Lindsey.**

Lina Short for **Adelina** or **Carolina**—or for **Adeline** or **Caroline.**

Lincoln a surname deriving from the English cathedral-city, is, in the U.S.A., bestowed as a 'Christian' in honour of that great man, Abraham Lincoln (1809-65).

Linda familiarly **Lindy** Either a short form of **Belinda** and **Melinda** and other **-linda** names, or adopted from Ger. **Linda.**

Lindsay (predominantly Scots) ; **Lindsey** (predominantly English), strictly surnames, the latter probably from **Lindsey,** a division of Lincolnshire. Both : m. and f.

Lionel Fr. for 'little lion'.

Lise A shortening of **Elise;** a variation of **Liza;** a variation of **Louise.**

Liz, Lizzie Pet-forms of **Elizabeth.**

Liza From **Eliza.**

Llew The Welsh answer to **Les.**

Llewellyn m. From Celtic, it means 'lion-like'.

Lloyd m. From the Celtic for 'grey'. Especially common in Wales.

Lodowick m. A Scottish name corresponding to the English **Ludovick;** ultimately akin to **Lewis.**

Lois f. When from **Aloisia** or **Héloïse,** it is properly **Loïs;** when of one syllable, it comes from the Heb. for 'better'.

Lola f. Originally Spanish, it pet-forms **Dolores.**

Lolly See **Laura.**

Lora The pet-name for **Leonora.**

Lorn m., represents that **Loarn** who with Angus and Fergus led the migration from Ireland to Scotland.

Lorna, or **Lorne** is a f. name of A.S. origin. It has the same meaning as 'love-lorn', i.e. lost.

Lothair From Frankish **Lothar,** 'famous warrior'. Also **Lothar** and **Lowther.**

Lothario A doublet of **Lothair.**

Lottie, Lotty The pet-form of **Charlotte.**

Lou A diminutive of both **Louis** and **Louisa.** Cf. **Lew.**

Louis As an English name, it is much less frequent than **Lewis.**

Louisa The English f. of the preceding. Cf. :

Louise Properly, the Fr. f. of **Louis**.

Lu A diminutive of all the **Lu**-names except **Luke**.

Lucas m. See **Luke**.

Lucia See **Lucy**.

Lucian L. **Lucianus**, a translation of Gr. **Loukianos**.

Lucilla, Lucille From St **Lucilla**, diminutive of **Lucia**.

Lucius A common L. name '(one) born at daylight'.

Lucy Probably the English representation of Fr. **Lucie**, from L. **Lucia** (occasionally used in English), the f. of **Lucius**.

Ludo Diminutive of **Ludovic** or **Ludovick**—see **Lodowick**.

Luke Gr. **Loukas** becomes L. **Lucas**, whence Fr. **Luc**, E. **Luke;** the name signifies 'he of Lucania'.

Lulu f. Diminutive of **Louise** (-sa).

Luther From the Ger. surname **Luther**.

Lydia Gr., 'a woman of Lydia'.

Lynn occasionally **Lyn**. Perhaps from Celtic for 'a lake'.

M

Mabel is short for **Amabel**.

Macaire An Irish m., it is probably an adaptation of the Gr. **Makarios**, probably in its L. form, **Macarius**, especially as there were, in C4, two notable saints so named.

Macbeth Drawn from Celtic, It means 'son of life'.

Maddie A diminutive of:

Madeline An English variant of **Magdalen(e)**; cf. the Fr. **Madeleine**.

Madge A splendidly English reshaping of **Margaret**.

Madison Properly a surname. Used mostly in the United States.

Madoc m. Probably a personification of Welsh madawg, 'strong and handsome'.

Mae is an affected form of **May**.

Magda is a shortening of **Magdalena**, the Ger. form of:

Magdalen, **Magdalene** (rare). Heb., '(the woman) of Magdala', that city on the shores of the Sea of Galilee which is famed as the birthplace of Mary Magdalene.

Maggie, **Maggy** A pet-form of **Margaret**.

Magnus See **Manus**.

Maida f. From the battle of Maida (in Italy), 1806.

Maidie See **Maisie**. It is also a diminutive of **Maida**.

Maisie, **Maidie** Scottish diminutives of **Margaret**.

Malachi, **-chy** Usually m., It is also, in late C19-20, occasionally f. In Heb., '(God's) messenger'.

Malcolm Originally **Maelcolum**, 'a disciple of Columb'.

Mall A sensible English contraction of **Matilda**.

Mamie is strictly a diminutive of **Margaret**.

Mandy is the diminutive of **Amanda**.

Manus m. From L. magnus, 'great'. **Magnus** itself is not uncommon in Scotland and the Scottish isles.

Marcella. The f. of **Marcellus,** adopted from **L.** where it is the diminutive of **Marcus,** q.v.

Marcia The f. of:

Marcius A L. shape (from **Marcus**) of **Mark.**

Marco The It. for **Mark;** occasionally used as a pet-name.

Marcus This L. name, probably deriving from **Mars,** god of war, is also a variant of **Mark:** from Gr. **Markos.**

Margaret This, one of the best of our English f. 'Christians', derives from Gr. margarites, 'a pearl'. English variants are **Margaretta, Margery, Mag, Maggie, Meggie, Madge, Marget, Peggy, Greta, Gritty, Meta;** Scottish, **Marjorie** (now also English), **Maisie, Maidie, May** (likewise), **Margie** and **Meg.**

Margery An English spelling of **Marjorie, -y.**

Margot A Fr. shortening of **Marguerite.**

Marguerite Originally the Fr. form of **Margaret.** Less popular is the more English **Marigold,** another flower-name.

Mari The Irish form of **Maria, Mary.**

Maria For the origin, see **Mary, Maria.** The L., It., Sp. form, it was once in England a royal name. Pet-form: **Ria.**

Marian A variant, made in the Middle Ages, of **Marion.**

Mariana A Spanish form of **Maria;** an English of **Mary.**

Marianne Originally, a Fr. name. Lit., **Mary Anne.**

Maribelle 'lovely Mary' **(la belle Marie)** is fanciful.

Marie is properly the Fr. form of **Maria** and therefore the perfect equivalent of our English **Mary,** but its correct pronunciation is so pleasant as to justify its adoption by the generous-minded Briton.

Marigold See **Marguerite.**

Marilyn See **Marylyn.**

Marina derives from L. **Maria.**

Marion In mid C19-20, more general than **Marian;** a diminutive of Fr. **Marie.**

Maris m. A Scottish offshoot from **Mary.**

Marius L., 'of Mars' : an old Roman name.

Marjorie, Marjory A variant of **Margaret.** Diminutives: **Marge, Margie.**

Mark From L. **Marcus** (q.v.). To the early Christian Church it was familiar as **Markos.** The Church has, in fact, done much to spread the name.

Marmaduke m. Of Celtic origin, it may mean 'servant of Madoc'. Diminutive **Duke.**

Marta, Martita Of these two f. names, the former is a variant, the latter a diminutive, of **Martha.**

Martha Aramaean, 'lady'.

Martie, Marty A diminutive of **Martha.**

Martin L. **Martinus,** from **Martius,** 'of Mars'; hence, perhaps, 'a disciplinarian'.

Martina The f. of **Martin, Marcus,** and **Mark.**

Mary The English shape of **Maria.** The earliest form is **Miriam,** a variant of the Heb. **Mariam(ne),** whence **Maria.**
　The two possible Heb. radicals of **Mary** and **Miriam** signify 'to be fat' and 'to be rebellious'. As Dr Cooke, former Regius Professor of Hebrew at Oxford, remarks, 'No new-born child would be called "rebellious" by its mother. "Fat, plump" might well be a name bestowed by a gratified parent. In the East fatness was, and is, admired as an element of female beauty'. Diminutives : **May, Moll(y), Poll(y).**

Marylyn or **Marilyn** f., is connected with **Mary,** of which it may be a diminutive. Cf. the Ger. **Marlene,** the Irish **Maureen.**

Mat The usual diminutive of **Matthew.**

Matilda Teutonic, 'might of battle'. Diminutives: **Matt(y), Patty, Tilly.**

Matthew The Heb. **Mattithyah,** 'gift of the Lord', became L. **Matthaeus** and **Matthias;** therefore **Matthew** and **Matthias** are doublets.

Matthias See preceding.

Mattie usually **Matty.** A pet-form of the preceding (contrast **Mat**) and of **Matilda.**

Maud, Maude An English derivative, via Old Fr., of Ger. **Mahthildis,** modern **Mathilde,** English **Matilda.** Pet-form: **Maudie.**

Maura variant, **Moira.** From Late L. **Maria**—see **Mary.** Diminutive: **Maureen.** All three—**Maura, Moira, Maureen**— were originally and still are predominantly Irish.

Maureen variant, **Maurine.** See preceding.

Maurice m. See **Morrice, Morris.** As a given name, **Maurice** is the more frequent.

Maurine See **Maureen.**

Mavis f. From Fr.; lit., 'song thrush'.

Max. The usual diminutive of the next.

Maxim; Maximilian respectively L. maximus, 'greatest', and L. **Maxim(us Aem)ilianus,** 'greatest Aemilianus', most important man in the gens **Aemilia.** It has for centuries been a favourite with European royalty and aristocracy.

Maxwell Properly a surname.

May A contraction of both **Mary** and **Margaret;** not a flower-name, nor yet a month-name.

Meara m. From Celtic mear, 'merry'.

Meg, Meggie or **Meggy** Diminutives of **Margaret**.

Mehetabel or **Mehitabel** Heb., 'God makes (us) happy'.

Melanie From the f. (melaina) of the Gr. mélas, 'black'—hence, 'dark-complexioned'. The present form is adopted from the Fr. Mélanie. Diminutive, **Mel**. **Melanie** is sometimes spelt **Meloney** or **Mellon(e)y**, especially in the United States.

Melinda demands quotation from the ever-delightful **Jack and Jill**: 'The later Stuarts had rather a craze for names in -inda, such as Clarinda, Dorinda, Florinda, Melinda, perhaps suggested by Ariosto's Belinda'. Now, -lind 'is usually Old German lind, snake . . . It is a common ending in German female names.'

Melissa Gr. melissa, 'a bee', hence 'honey'.

Melody f. An English rural name—and a beautiful.

Melva m. Celtic, 'chief'.

Melvin m. Rare in Britain, fairly common in U.S.A. Perhaps formed from **Melva**.

Menzies A Scottish shortening and reshaping of **Clemence**. In C20 more common as surname than as font-name.

Mercedes This Sp. name arises from **Maria de las Mercedes**, (Virgin) Mary of the Mercies.

Mercia A.S. 'woman from the border-lands'.

Mercy f. One of the virtue-names: cf. **Patience**.

Meredith m. Welsh, 'sea-protector'.

Meriel A variant of **Muriel**.

Merle f. Modern, and more general in America than in England, it is Fr. merle, a blackbird.

Merlin Welsh **Myrddin**, perhaps 'sea-hill'.

Mervin, Mervyn m. (Diminutive: **Merv.**) An old Anglo-Saxon name: **Maerwine**, 'famous friend'.

Meta An occasional diminutive of **Margaret.**

Meyrick From Teutonic, 'work-ruler'.

Michael In Heb., 'who (is) like to God?' As with **John** and **Mark**, so with **Michael**: we now think of it as an essentially British name.

Mick, Micky, Mike Diminutives of **Michael.**

Mildred occasionally **Mildrid.** The A.S. **Mildthryth** means either 'mild power' or 'mild counsel'.

Miles, Myles the Irish form. The name has now one, now another, origin: (1) **Michael**, in Fr. **Mihiel** or **Miel**, yields **Miles**; (2) 'Milo, the strong man of Crotona, was adopted very early in French . . . Its Old French nominative was Miles.'

Milicent, Millicent Teutonic, 'work-strong'. The modern Fr. form **Mélisande** occasionally appears in C20 English, with or without the accent.

Millie or **Milly** A diminutive of **Emily** and **Mil(l)icent.**

Mina This is an English pet-form of **Wilhelmina.**

Minna A Scottish variant of:

Minnie f. Ger. **Minne**, 'love'.

Mirabel occasionally elaborated to **Mirabella.** This f. derives from L. mirabilis, 'wonderful'.

Miranda L., 'worthy of admiration'.

Miriam is probably the earliest form of **Mary.**

Moggy, Moke Variants of **Molly.**

Moira f. Celtic, 'soft'. Sometimes a variant of **Maura.**

Moll, Molly Diminutives of **Mary.**

Mona f. Sometimes '(a girl) of or from Mona'; sometimes from the Irish **Muadhnait**, diminutive of muadh, 'noble'.

Monica f., may cast back to Gr. monos, f. mone, 'alone' or 'unique'.

Montagu(e) m., is a 'Christianizing' of the surname, which represents Fr. mont aigu, a (sharply) peaked hill.

Monty The diminutive of the preceding.

Morgan m. From the Celtic for 'a sea-dweller'.

Morgana The f. of **Morgan**.

Morna From **Muirne**, Gaelic for 'affection'.

Morrice, Morris, Maurice Probably from L. **Mauritius**, a Proper Name formed from **Maurus**, 'a Moor'.

Mort, Mortie or **Morty** Diminutives of **Mortimer**.

Mortimer Sometimes from Celtic, 'sea-warrior'; sometimes from a Fr. place-name.

Morvryn m. This Welsh name means 'sea-king'.

Moses This grand old Jewish name perhaps derives from Egyptian rather than from Hebrew. Pet-form: **Mo**.

Moyna See **Mona** (at end).

Mungo m. In Celtic, 'lovable; beloved'.

Murdoch m. A Scottish variant of **Murtoch**.

Muriel Probably from Old Irish **Muirgheal**, it means 'sea-bright'; perhaps diminutive from Gr. murrha, myrrh.

Murray m. A 'Christianizing' of the surname.

Murtagh; Murtoch m. The Irish and the Scottish forms of a name that, deriving from the Celtic, means 'sea-protector'— 'sea-warrior'—'sea man; seaman'.

Myfanwy, Myvanwy f. From Celtic, either mabanwy, 'child of the water', or my-manwy, 'my fine (or rare) one'.

Myles An Irish variant of **Miles.**

Myra less frequently, **Mira.** Either variants of **Muriel** or, more probably, short for **Miranda.**

Myrtilla A diminutive of **Myrtle,** it is often bestowed as an independent name.

Myrtle comes from Fr. **myrtille,** 'bilberry', a diminutive of myrte, myrtle, itself via L. from Gr. murtos. Pet-name: **Myrt.**

N

Nadine f. Russian **Nadezna,** 'Hope'.

Nahum m. Heb., '(a source of) comfort'.

Nan A diminutive of **Anne** or **Hannah.** Its own diminutive **Nanette** has been adopted from Fr.

Nancy Either a typically English metathesis of **Anne** or a variant of **Agnes,** perhaps influenced by the It. **Nanna,** a diminutive of **Anna,** and Ger. **Annchen,** likewise a diminutive.

Naomi Heb., '(my) pleasant (one)'.

Napoleon It., 'one who belongs to the new city': Gr. neapolis: Naples. Pet-name: **Nap.**

Nat, Natty Diminutives of **Nathan** and **Nathaniel.**

Natalia, Natalie f. L. natalis, 'natal'.

Nathan Heb., 'a gift'. Cf.:

Nathaniel Heb., 'gift of God'.

Neal In Celtic, 'a champion'. Cf. **Nelson**.

Ned A diminutive, like **Ed** and **Ted**, of **Edward**.

Neil, Neill The former a mere spelling-variant of the latter, which parallels **Niul**, the original of **Neal**.

Nell, Nellie Diminutives of **Helen, Ellen, Eleanor(a)**, but often bestowed independently.

Nelson Its use as a baptismal name dates from 1798-1805, the period of the great English admiral's victories. **Nelson** is 'son of **Nell**'; and this **Nell** is a variant of **Neal**, q.v. (Reaney.)

Nessa, Nessie, Nesta. Celtic diminutives of **Agnes**. The first and the second: also of **Vanessa**.

Netta See **Nita**.

Neville Strictly a surname, of Fr. origin (**Neuville**; lit., the new city); introduced by the Normans. Pet-form: **Nev**.

Nial or **Niall** is a Celtic m. name; it means 'a champion'. Cf. both **Neal** and **Nelson** above.

Nicholas occasionally **Nicolas**. From L. Nicolaus, Gr. Nikolaos, 'victory of the people'.

Nick; Nicky Diminutives of **Nicholas**.

Nicol or **Nichol** A mainly Scottish shortening of **Nicholas**.

Niel A Scottish form of **Neal**.

Nigel From L. niger, 'black'—perhaps with a reminiscence of pre-Classical L. nigellus, 'somewhat black'.

Nina Originally a pet-form of **Anna** (or **Anne**), via Fr. **Nanine**, itself from **Anne**.

Nita A charming girl's name, deriving ultimately from L. nitidus, bright, neat. **Netta** is a doublet showing French influence. Often, however, it shortens either **Anita** or Sp. **Juanita**.

Noah Heb., 'rest'. It survives mainly in U.S.A. and the English countryside.

Noel Adopted from Fr. **Noel**; noël being Christmas, it derives from L. natalis, 'natal'.

Noll A pet-form of **Oliver.**

Nona L. nona, 'the ninth (female child)'.

Nora, Norah A mainly Irish name, earlier **Onora,** a Hibernicism for **Honora** or **Honoria.** Also short for **Eleanora** and **Leonora.**

Norbert Teutonic, 'Niord's brightness'.

Noreen A diminutive, originally Irish **(Noirin),** of **Nora.**

Norma f., comes from the L. norma, a pattern, a norm, but via Bellini's famous opera (1830), as I learn from **Jack and Jill.**

Norman Lit., 'a Northman'—i.e., a Norwegian; hence, from the settlement in N.W. France, a Norman. Pet-form: **Norm.**

Nowell A very English form of **Noel.**

O

Obadiah Heb. 'servant of the Lord'; diminutive, **Obie.**

Octavia, Octavius In L., 'the eighth daughter, son', respectively; L. octavus, 'eighth'.

Odette A diminutive of:

Odile f. Properly and mainly Fr., but, like the Ger. form, **Odila,** it is of Teutonic origin: '(she of) the fatherland'. Given its correct pronunciation (o-deel), it is attractive.

Olga f., comes, via Russian, from Norse **Helga**, 'holiness'.

Olive (See **Olivia** and **Oliver**.) This f. should be compared with **Daisy, Lily, Myrtle, Poppy, Rhoda, Rose, Rosemary, Violet**.

Oliver m. The English shape of Fr. **Olivier**, It. **Oliviero**, not necessarily from L. oliva, 'the olive'.

Olivia The Italianate original of **Olive**.

Ollie An occasional diminutive of **Olive** and a frequent diminutive of **Oliver**.

Ophelia Gr. ophelia, 'assistance'.

Orlando Originally It., this is a doublet of Fr. **Roland**.

Orson m. An English variation of Fr. ourson, a bear's cub, from ours (L. ursus), a bear.

Osbert m., like the Ger. f. **Osberta**, derives from the Teutonic and means 'divinely bright'.

Oscar This is the O.E. **Osgar**, 'divine spear'.

Osmond, Osmund This m. name signifies 'divine protection' and represents the Norwegian **Asmundr**.

Osric m. In Teutonic, 'divine rule or power'.

Ossie The pet-name for **Osbert, Osmond, Oswald**.

Oswald comes from A.S. **Osweald**, 'divine power'.

Otto As a Ger. name, it means 'rich'; as an It. name, a contraction of **Ottavio**, 'the eighth' (see **Octavia, Octavius**).

Owen now almost as English as it is Welsh, and a surname as well as a 'Christian'. Of Celtic origin; perhaps meaning 'youthful warrior'.

P

Paddy A familiar form of **Patrick. Cf. Pat** and **Patsy.**

Padraic A more 'national' form of Irish **Patrick.**

Pamela Probably derived from Gr. pan meli, 'all honey'.

Pat The most used diminutive of **Patrick;** the usual diminutive of **Patricia. Cf. Patsy** and **Paddy.**

Patience From L. patientia, it achieved a vogue among the Puritans and is still fairly common in English rural districts. Diminutive: **Patty.**

Patricia The f. of **Patrick** has been influenced, socially by its etymological sense ('patrician').

Patrick L. patricius, 'a patrician, a nobleman'; patricia comes from pater. **Patrick** has, in C18-20, been by far the commonest m. 'Christian' in Ireland.

Paul comes from L. paulus, 'little, small'. It owes its popularity to the Biblical Paul.

Paula The f. of **Paul.**

Pauline The diminutive of **Paula.** Pet-name: **Paulie.**

Pearl f. A jewel-name.

Peg A shortened form of:

Peggoty and **Peggy** Diminutives of **Margaret.**

Pelham Strictly a surname. Pet-forms: **Pel** and **Plum.**

Penelope Gr., 'a weaver'; diminutives, **Penny** and **Pen.**

Perce The pet-name for the next two.

Perceval in C19-20, generally **Percival.** 'The much discussed Perceval, Percival is simply what it appears to be, viz. 'pierce vale'. (Weekley, Surnames).

Percy Originally a surname, it comes from Fr. perce-haie, 'pierce-hedge'.

Peregrine m., is the L. peregrinus, 'a wanderer'.

Perpetua (L., 'everlasting, enduring') is a Catholic f., commemorating the C3 virgin martyr. Diminutive **Peppi**.

Perry The diminutive of **Peregrine**.

Pete A mainly American shortening of:

Peter Gr. petros, 'a stone', perhaps influenced by petra, 'a rock'—with the implication 'firm as a rock': 'Thou art **Petros** (a stone), and on this **Petra** (a rock) I will build my Church,' said Christ.

Petrina and **Petronella** or **-illa** The former is the direct f. of **Peter**; the latter, a diminutive of **Petronia,** the f. of L. **Petronius,** perhaps from petra, 'a stone'.

Phil A diminutive of **Philip, Philippa, Phyllis.**

Philemon m. Gr., 'loving, friendly'.

Philip Gr. **Philippos,** 'fond of horses'. The Apostle Philip and Philip the Deacon; French and Spanish kings; noblemen innumerable; famous writers: all have contributed to spread **Philip** (etc.) throughout Europe.

Philippa The English f. of the preceding.

Phineas m., is of fiercely disputed origin and waning use.

Phoebe As Phoebus is the sun-god (Apollo), so Phoebe is the moon-goddess (Artemis; Roman Diana); they derive from the m. and f. of the Gr. adjective for 'radiant' or 'bright'. Pet-form: **Phebe** (one syllable).

Phyllida A variant of **Phyllis.**

Phyllis occasionally **Phillis** From Gr. phullis, genitive phullidis, 'a green leaf' or 'bough'.

Pierce A Fr., hence an English and Irish form of **Peter.**

Piers An early contraction—from the Fr.—of **Peter.**

Pip A diminutive of **Philip**, as Ian Hay's delightful **Pip**, a Romance of Youth makes abundantly clear.

Plum See **Pelham**.

Polly A pet-form of **Mary**, just as **Molly** is.

Pompey L. **Pompeius**, '(a man) of Pompeii'. The name owes much to Pompey the Great, the Triumvir; scourge of pirates, conqueror of Mithridates.

Poppy is a f. flower-name.

Portia This f., of pretty Shakespearean memory, reshapes L. **Porcia**, a female member of the great gens **Porcia** or Porcian clan.

Primrose f. A flower-name, lit. 'first, or early, bloom'.

Priscilla The diminutive of L. prisca, the f. of priscus, 'olden' or 'ancient'. Pet-name: **Prissy**.

Prosper L. prosper or prosperus, 'fortunate' or 'prosperous'.

Pru, Prue Diminutive of:

Prudence Cf. L. **Prudentia**, f. of **Prudentius**, from prudens, 'discreet', 'prudent'. It became popular among the Puritans.

Pugh This Celtic m. 'Christian' contracts Welsh **Ap Hu**, lit. 'son of Hew (or Hu)'.

Q

Queenie This f. probably derives from queen.

Quentin or **Quintin** In L., **Quintus** ('the fifth') was a very common fore-name; there was, moreover, a Quintian 'gens' or clan.

R

Rab The Scottish equivalent to **Rob**. Whence **Rabbie**.

Rachel Heb., 'a ewe', emblematic of gentleness.

Rafe is merely a phonetic representation of the fashionable pronunciation of:

Ralf usually **Ralph** The O.E. raedwulf, lit. 'counsel (of) wolf', became **Radulf**, which became **Ralf**; it corresponds to the Fr. **Raoul**.

Ranald A variant of **Ronald**.

Randal or **Randle** comes from **Randolf**. Pet-name: **Ran.**

Randolf now always **Randolph** the sense is 'shield-wolf' or 'house-wolf'. The spelling **Randolph** results from the Latinized **Radulphus** and the surname form, **Randolph**. Pet-name: **Randy.**

Raphael Heb., 'the medicine of God; God's healing'.

Ray As m., it was originally the diminutive of **Raymond**; as f., **Ray** baffles me, unless it is simply the **Ra-** of **Rachel** or short for the Fr. f. **Raymonde**.

Raymond Old Frankish **Raginmund**, 'wise or, powerful protection'.

Rebecca, Rebekah Heb., 'a snare' (lit. 'a noosed cord') from rabak, 'to bind'.

Redmond Teutonic, 'counsel- or council-protection'.

Reece The English form of **Rhys**.

Reg, Reggie Diminutives of **Reginald** and:

Regina Direct from L., where it means 'queen'.

Reginald Teutonic, 'judgement-power' or 'counsel-power or ruler' is taken to mean 'powerful judgement'.

Rene A shortening of **Irene**.

Reuben Heb., 'behold, a son!' Diminutive: **Rube**.

Rex is not always L. rex, 'a king'—sometimes it 'telescopes' **Reginald**.

Rhoda, Rhode (rare). Gr. rhoda, 'roses'; rhode, 'a rose-bush'; these indicate the origin.

Rhys This very general Welsh m. is pronounced **Reece**. Rhys, in Welsh, is 'an impetuous man or warrior'.

Rice An English form of **Rhys**.

Rick Pet-name for **Eric**.

Richard comes, via Old Fr., from Teutonic for 'rule hard', i.e. 'stern ruler or king'. The diminutives are **Diccon** (obsolete), **Rick** (obsolescent), **Ritchie**, and **Dick**. Like **Robert**, it is one of the best and most popular names.

Rina A diminutive of **Katharine**.

Rita is a diminutive, either of **Margarita** or of It. **Margherita**.

Ritchie A Scottish diminutive of **Richard**.

Rob Properly the original of **Robin**, **Rob** was at first, and sometimes even now, a diminutive of **Robert**.

Robert Teutonic, 'bright fame', anciently **Hrodebert**: hrod or hrothi, fame+bertha, bright. Honoured in both France and Germany, he became Ruprecht in the latter, and Robert in the former. Pet-names: **Rob, Robbie,** or in Scots, **Rab, Rabbie; Bob; Robin**.

Roberta is the f. form of **Robert**.

Robin Originally a diminutive of **Rob**; but, ever since C12, predominantly an independent name. It owes some of its popularity to the legends of **Robin Goodfellow** and **Robin Hood**.

Robina rarely, **Robinia**. The f. of **Robin**.

Rod, Roddy Diminutives of **Roderic** and **Rodney.**

Roderic, Roderick Northern **Hrothrekr,** Old Ger. **Hrodric,** lit. 'fame rule'—hence 'famous ruler'.

Rodney m., is a 'Christianizing' of the surname, popularized by the famous C18 admiral, Lord Rodney.

Rodolph occ. **Rodolf.** Teutonic, 'wolf-fame'. Likewise, **Rudolf** is a variant, properly and mainly Ger., as is **Rudolph,** from the Fr. form, **Rodolphe.**

Roger comes, via Old Fr., from the Teutonic for 'fame-spear'; earliest forms O.E. **Hrothgar** and Old Ger. **Hrodgar.** Pet-name! **Rog.**

Roland is lit. 'land-fame': Old Ger. **Hrodland.** A certain knight slain at Roncesvalles in the days of Charlemagne was celebrated in the Old Fr. epic known as the 'Chanson de Roland'. Diminutives: **Rolly** and **Roly.**

Rolf, Rolph occasionally **Rolfe.** See **Rodolph.**

Rollo A transformation of **Rodolph.**

Roma whence (?) **Romer** It is either a contraction of **Romola** or, more probably, a direct personification of **Roma,** the L. original of **Rome,** the city.

Rona appears to be the f. of:

Ronald like the English **Reynold,** is a variation of **Reginald.** Diminutives: **Ron, Ronnie.**

Roosevelt a surname of Dutch extraction (roos, a rose+veld, a field: compare veld roos, a wild rose), has, since ca. 1905, graced many a young American hopeful.

Rorie, Rory This Irish m. comes from a Celtic radical meaning 'red' or 'ruddy'.

Rosa See **Rose.**

Rosabel, Rosabella The latter is merely rosa bella, 'pretty rose'— with **Rosabel** as an Anglicism.

Rosalia now rare; Rosalie Formed from L. rosalis, rosy, rose-like.

Rosalind, Rosalinda (now rare) **Rosaline.** 'Fair as a rose'¡ Rosa+linda, as in Sp. linda, '(a) pretty (woman)'.

Rosamond, Rosamund The former varies the latter, which occurs first as **Rosamunda,** 'horse-protection'; has been wrongly associated with **Rosa.**

Rosanna, Rosanne Combinations of **Rosa** and **Anna** (or **Anne**).

Rosa, Rose Certainly the C15-20 **Rosa** and **Rose,** whatever their dim-distant origin, are to be referred to the burgeoning and the full-blown rose, the latter so often symbolic. In short, the very old L.-from-Gr. flower-name has absorbed several Teutonic names of 'fame' or 'nobility' origin.

Rosemary has, in its passage from the L. plant-name ros marinus, 'dew of the sea', whence Old Fr. rosmarin, been influenced by **Mary.**

Rosetta, Rosina The English and the Italian-become-English pet-form of **Rose.**

Rosie A diminutive of **Rosa, Rose, Rosamund, Rosetta, Rosina, Rosemary.**

Ross Properly a surname.

Rowena Originally **Rhonwen.** Welsh for 'white skirt'. The name received fresh life from the Rowena of Scott's 'Ivanhoe', 1819.

Rowland An English variant of **Roland.**

Roy Probably from the Celtic for 'red'.

Rube A familiar pet-name for **Reuben.**

Ruby A 'jewel-name' like **Beryl, Emerald, Pearl.**

Rudolf, Rudolph See **Rodolph.**

Ruby The diminutive of **Rudolph.**

Rue The pet-form of **Ruth.**

Rufus L. rufus, 'red-haired'.

Rupert was originally, and still is, a Ger. m. name, **Ruprecht** or **Rupprecht**, earlier **Hruodebert, Hrodebert,** which designates '(one for whom) bright fame (is hoped)'. It is a doublet of **Robert.** Pet-name **Rupe.**

Russell m. More common as a surname, **Russell** Anglicizes the Old French **Roussel,** 'the Red-Head'. Pet-name: **Russ.**

Ruth Heb., but whether 'trembling' or 'uniting' or 'friend' or, better, 'beauty' (or 'vision of beauty') we do not know.

S

Sabina f., represents L. **Sabina,** 'a Sabine woman'.

Sabrin (now rare), **Sabrina** It is, as **Sabrina**—for **Sabrin** is a curtailment—a Latinized and poetical name for the River Severn; hence a nymph haunting the Severn.

Sacheverell m. This uncommon 'Christian' derives from the surname, itself probably from the Fr. village of Saint-Chevreuil-du-Tronchet.

Sadie A pet-name for **Sarah** and, in the Dominions, occasionally bestowed as an independent font-name.

Sal, Sally The former is short for the latter, which anglicizes the Hebraic **Sarah.**

Salome Heb., 'peace'.

Sam, Sammy or **Sammie** Familiar forms of **Samuel.**

Sampson, Samson Heb., 'like the sun; resplendent'.

Samuel is, in Heb., 'heard of God'.

Sanchia f. Provençal and Sp. **Sanchia or Sancha,** from **L.** sanctus, 'holy, saintly'.

Sanders A Scottish re-shaping of **Alexander.**

Sandra is of It. origin. From **Alessandra (our Alexandra).**

Sandy A diminutive of **Sanders,** hence of **Alexander.**

Sapphira Gr. sappheiros, 'the lapis lazuli or sapphire'.

Sara, Sarah The Heb. **Sarai,** 'the quarrelsome', became **Sarah,** 'the princess' (from sar, 'a prince').

Saul Heb. 'asked for'.

Saunders A Scottish transformation of **Alexander**—therefore cf. **Sanders.**

Savy An Irish diminutive of **Xavier.**

Sawny A diminutive of **Sanders** and **Alexander.**

Seamus m. Incorrect spelling of **Seumas.**

Sean (Pronounced **Shawn.**) An Irish form of John.

Seba m. Rare in England; not uncommon in U.S.A. In origin, probably a shortening of:

Sebastian L. **Sebastianus,** a derivative of **Sebastos,** 'the venerated; majestic'.

Selina Perhaps a confusion of Fr. **Céline,** Gr. **Selene,** the moon-goddess.

Septimus L., 'the seventh (boy)'.

Serena From L. serenus, calm or untroubled.

Seth Heb., 'appointed'; perhaps 'compensation'.

Seumas The Irish form of **James.** Cf.:

Shamus An Anglicized form of **Seumas.**

Shan or Shane The English spelling of **Séan,** itself an Irish form of **John.**

Sheelah, She(e)lagh A contraction of **Sighile.**

Sheila The English form of the preceding.

Shirley A girl's name not much used before the late C19.
From the surname, itself from an English place-name. Pet-form:
Shirl.

Sholto was adopted as a name in the Douglas family, and crept
from thence to others; of Celtic origin.

Si Short for **Simon** and **Silas.**

Sibyl; Sybil Gr. sibulla, 'a Sybil', 'a prophetess', and, derivatively,
L. sibylla, show the correct spelling.

Sid The diminutive of:

Sidney, Sydney Both m. and, though less often, f. Like **Howard**
and **Percy,** it is properly a surname.

Sighile 'In Ireland, the Norman settlers introduced (**Cecilia**), and
it became Sighile'. Yonge.

Silas derives, by contraction from L. **Silvanus,** the god of forests.
Diminutive: **Si.**

Silvan, Silvanus See **Sylvanus; Silvan** is a shortening.

Silvester from the L. silvestris, 'belonging to a forest'.

Silvia See **Sylvia.**

Silvie A pet-name for any **Sylvia.**

Sim The 'endearment' of the next. Diminutive: **Simmie.**

Simeon Heb., 'obedient; hearkening'. Already in C1 A.D. had
Simeon been confused with:

Simon In Gr., **Simon** is 'the snub-nose', but as a New Testament
name it seems to have been a mere Grecism for **Simeon.**
Diminutive: **Si.**

Sis, Sissie Variants of **Cis, Cissie:** see **Cicely.**

Sisley An English variant of **Cicely**.

Sol, Solly Diminutives of :

Solomon This Heb. name means 'the peaceable'.

Sonia From Slavonic, it means 'wise one'. Akin to :

Sophia, Sophy Gr. sophia, 'wisdom' ; **Sophy**, from Fr. **Sophia** (also used).

Sorcha f. An Irish name, from Celtic for 'bright'.

Stacey, Stacy f. and m. An English contraction of **Anastasia** and **Anastacius**.

Stan The diminutive of **Stanley** and :

Stanislas, Stanislaus From a Russian name, meaning 'martial glory'.

Standish Probably from the surname **Standish**.

Stanley was originally, like **Howard, Percy, Sidney**, a very aristocratic surname.

Stella From L. stella, 'a star'. Pet-form : **Stell**.

Stephanie The f. of **Stephen**.

Stephen sometimes Anglicized as **Steven**. Gr. **Stephanos** personifies stephanos, a garland, a wreath, especially as used for a crown. Diminutive : **Steve**.

Sue is the pet-form of **Susan** and **Susanna(h)**.

Susan The English shortening of **Susanna**.

Susanna or **Susannah** In Heb., it is 'graceful white lily'.

Susie A diminutive of **Susan** and **Susanna(h)**.

Suzanne is properly the Fr. shape of **Susanna**. Pet-name : **Suze** or **Suse**.

Sybil See **Sibyl**.

Sydney See **Sidney**.

Sylvan See **Silvan**.

Sylvanus, Silvanus which, when any L. allusion is intended, is the correct spelling; otherwise, **Sylvanus** is usual. Silvanus was a divinity of the fields and forests.

Sylvester Like the preceding, it is a m. equivalent of **Sylvia**. See also **Silvester**.

Sylvia, Silvia 'Who is Sylvia, what is she?' as the song goes in The Two Gentlemen of Verona. Apparently, one who lives in a wood (L. silva).

T

Tabitha Lit., in Aramaic, 'gazelle'.

Tad An American diminutive of **Thady** (or **Thaddeus**) and, only among Irish-Americans, of:

Taffy A Welsh diminutive of **David**.

Tafline The Welsh f. of **David**.

Talbot Properly a surname.

Tam, Tammie Scottish diminutives of **Thomas**.

Tancred From Teutonic for 'thought-strong'.

Tania or Tanya Of Roman origin, it is a diminutive of **Natalia**.

Teague m. As an Irish 'Christian', it is a degeneration from **Tadhgh**.

Ted, Teddy Transformations of **Edward**; the latter, also a diminutive of **Theodore**.

Terence The Anglicizing of L. **Terentius**, the name of a celebrated writer of comedy and of the Terential Clan.

Teresa is now the usual form of a f. which, in its Gr. original, indicates 'a reaper' (lit., 'carrying ears of corn').

Terry A diminutive of both **Terence** and **Teresa** (**Theresa**).

Tess, Tessa, Tessie Diminutives of **Teresa**.

Thaddeus Late L. **Thaddaeus**: Gr. **Thaddaios**, of disputed origin.

Thady The commonest variant of the preceding.

Thecla, Thekla In Gr., 'divine fame'.

Theo A diminutive of all the names in **Theo-**.

Theobald In C19-20, mainly a surname; in Teutonic it signifies 'folk-bold'.

Theodora The f. of :

Theodore Gr. **Theodoros**, L. **Theodorus**, Fr. **Théodore**, Ger. **Theodor**, it means 'God's gift'; in **Dorothea(-y)** the order is reversed to 'gift of God'.

Theodoric, Theodric In Teutonic, 'people's ruler'.

Theodosia Like **Theodora**, 'divine gift'.

Theophilus Gr. **Theophilos**, 'beloved of God'.

Theresa This is the more traditional, but now less usual, English form of **Teresa**.

Thirzah, Tirzah f. Heb., 'pleasantness'. The variant **Thyrza** may sometimes be used for **Theresa**.

Thomas Lit., 'a twin'. Its popularity may be attributed to the prevalence of **Thomas** among the saints.

Thomasina (or -ssina); Thomas(s)ine The f. of the preceding.

Thorold is a Norwegian m. name (Thorald) naturalized in England. In Teutonic, it connotes 'Thor's rule'.

Thyrza See **Thirzah.**

Tib. A pet-form of **Isabel** cf. **Tibbie.**

Tibal, Tibble Pleasant English derivatives of **Theobald,** usually pronounced **Tibbald.**

Tibbie A Scottish pet-name for **Isabel.** Diminutive of **Tib.**

Tiernan From Celtic, it means 'kingly' (tighearn, a king); it has derivatives **Tiernay, Tierney.**

Tilda, Tilly The former is a shortening of **Matilda** and the second an endearing of **Tilda.**

Tim The shortening as **Timmie (-my)** is the diminutive, of the next.

Timothy Gr. **Timotheos,** L. **Timotheus,** Fr. **Timothée,** means, lit., 'honour God' (hence, 'honouring God').

Tina A diminutive of **Albertina, Christina, Ernestine.**

Tirzah See **Thirzah.**

Titus perhaps comes from Gr. tio, I honour.

Tobias. Heb., 'God is good'.

Toby An Anglicizing of **Tobias.**

Tolley or **Tolly** A pet-name for **Bartholomew.**

Tom The usual pet-form of **Thomas.**

Tommy A further endearing of **Thomas;** immediately, a diminutive of **Tom.**

Tony The pet-form of **Antony.** Occasionally **Tone.**

Tracy f. An English reshaping of **Theresa.** As m., it probably represents the surname **Tracey** or **Tracy,** which is of Fr. place-name origin. (Reaney.)

Trefor The Welsh form and original of **Trevor.**

Trevor A 'Christianizing' of the surname. Pet-form: **Trev.**

Tricia A pet-form of both **Beatrice** and **Patricia.**

Triffie, Triffy A diminutive of **Tryphaena.**

Trissie or **Trissy** See **Beatie.**

Tristram is probably akin to A.S. **Thurstan,** 'Thor's stone' (or jewel). A name famous in old romance and in modern opera.

Trix, Trixy See **Beatie.**

Truda, Trude Strictly pet-forms of **Gertrude.**

Tryphaena now usually **Tryphena.** Gr., 'delicious (female)', 'dainty (girl)'.

Tudor A Welsh reshaping of **Theodore.**

Tyrrell Strictly a surname a variant of **Tirrell,** which as Reaney suggests, is probably akin to the Fr. **Tirand,** 'one who pulls (Fr. tirer) in the reins', hence stubborn.

U

Ulric or **Ulrick** the latter being much the more usual. A Norman spelling of O.E. **Wulfric,** 'wolf-rule'.

Ulrica A f. derivative, originally Roman, of the preceding.

Ulysses is the L. shape of Gr. **Odusseus.**

Una Partly Irish **(Oonagh),** partly L. (una f. of unus, one).

Unity One of the abstract names, such as **Felicity, Mercy and Patience**: all bestowed on girls, not boys.

Ursula In 'L., 'little she-bear'.

Ursy, Ursie The diminutive of the preceding.

V

Val A diminutive of the next four names.

Valentine From L. **Valentinus**, a diminutive from valens, 'strong': for the origin, cf. **Valerius**.

Valerian m. The Anglicizing of L. **Valerianus**, the adjective corresponding to **Valerius**.

Valerie Adopted from the Fr. **(Valérie)**, itself from L. **Valeria**, the f. of:

Valerius L., 'healthy'. It derives from valere, to be strong, to be (so much) worth, and valour, value and courage.

Van The usual pet-form of the next two names.

Vanessa is a Latinizing of Van-+Esther; Van- was, in Heb., 'grace of God'.

Vanora Celtic, 'white wave'.

Vashti This f. name (diminutive: **Vassy**) is mostly Cornish: it derives from the Persian for 'star'.

Venetia In Celtic, 'blessed'; perhaps influenced by **Venus**.

Vera In Serbia, this f. 'Christian' means 'faith'; in England it usually derives from L., '(a) true (woman)'.

Vere m. An aristocratic name, probably direct from the surname de Vere: cf. 'Vere de Vere'.

Vernon is a happy name, for it signifies 'flourishing'. Pet-name: **Vern(e)**.

Veronica is probably a distortion of **Berenice**, a Macedonian form of Gr. **Pherenike**, bringer of victory, the **Bernice** of Acts, xxv.

Vi The diminutive of **Viola** and **Violet**.

Vic, Vicky Diminutives of the next two names, **Vic** being the more general for the former, **Vicky** for the latter.

Victor In L., 'the conqueror' (cf. **Vincent**).

Victoria Popularized in the Commonwealth by the accession of a queen so youthful that she captured the hearts, as well as the imagination, of an outwardly stolid, inwardly sentimental nation. The earliest Victoria was the Roman goddess of victory (cf. **Victor**).

Vida A Welsh f. of **David** In some instances, perhaps Sp. vida, life.

Vin, Vince, Vinny Diminutives of **Vincent**. **Vinny** (or **Viney**) also pet-forms **Lavinia**.

Vincent L. vincens, 'conquering', accusative vincentem.

Viney, Vinny See **Vin**.

Viola Originally, as still mainly, the It. form of **Violet**, from L. viola, the violet.

Violet The It. viola has diminutive violetta, which became violete in Old Fr., the Mod. Fr. being violette.

Virgie, Virgy A diminutive, generally for **Virginia**.

Virgil L. **Virgilius** or **Vergilius**, related to **virere**, to flourish, and ver, the Spring.

Virginia like **Virgil**, is related to Spring and all fair growing things.

Viv The usual diminutive of the next three names.

Vivian rarely f. From L. **Vivianus, Viviana,** from vivus, 'alive'.

Vivien mostly f. This was originally a French form of **Vivian,** of which the f. is **Vivienne.**

Vivyan A mainly C19-20 variant of **Vivian.**

W

Walburga f. A.-S. **Waldburga,** 'powerful protector'.

Waldo m. A Frankish name from Norse vald, 'power'.

Wallace Properly, a surname.

Wally The now usual pet-form of **Walter.**

Walt Another pet-form of **Walter.**

Walter This is the most notable of the names (mostly m.) based on a Teutonic word denoting 'power' or 'rule'.

Wanda f. Perhaps from Teutonic for 'shepherdess'; but probably from Old Ger. vand, 'stem, stock'.

Warren Teutonic, lit. 'a protecting friend'. Now commoner as surname than as given name.

Washington properly a surname from an English place-name, has, ever since 1776, been a fairly common American given name, in honour of George Washington (1732-99), statesman and first President.

Wat, Wattie Diminutives of **Walter.**

Webster is, properly, a surname.

Wenda, Wendy From Teutonic **Wendla,** 'wanderer'; **Wendy** form, popularized by J. M. Barrie in 1904.

Wilfred, Wilfrid from the A.S. **Wilfrith,** which means 'will-peace', i.e. 'resolute peace'; the first element (wil) is thus the same as in **William.** Pet-name: **Wilf.**

Wilhelmina A f. derivative from **William.**

Will A pleasant diminutive of **William.**

Willa is of Teutonic origin; it means 'resolute'.
Diminitive: **Will**

William The **Will** part of the name represents the Teutonic for 'resolution'; -iam, Teutonic helm as 'helmet': therefore, 'helmet of resolution'. It is the second commonest of all 'Christians' in England, only **John** beating it, though **Thomas** must run it very close. Diminutives: **Will, Willie; Bill, Billie.** Variants: **Willy** and **Billy.**

Willis is strictly a surname.

Wilmer m. Either from Ger. **Wilmar,** 'willing fame'—or, in Common Teutonic, 'willing warrior'.

Wilmot, m. Probably 'little William'.

Wilson comes from **Will's son.**

Win The usual diminutive of:

Winifred, Winifrid Earlier **Wenefrede, -fride,** it means, -fride, in Celtic, 'white wave or stream'.

Winne f. A Celtic name of Celtic origin ('white').

Winnie or **Winny** A diminutive of **Winifred.** Among the Irish, however, **Winny** pet-forms **Una.** Cf.:

Winston Properly a surname. Pet-form: **Winnie.**

Wyn An affected variant of **Win**; a natural but rare variant of **Winnie.** Occasionally used as m.

Xavier was originally a surname, gracing St Francis Xavier, a noble Spaniard famed for his missions in the 16th Century to India, Ceylon, the East Indies, Japan and China. Pet-name: **Xave** or, more usually, **Savy.**

Ysolt, Yseult; Isold, Isolda, Isolde From the Fr. **Yseulte,** perhaps from **Adsalutta,** a Celtic goddess.

Yvette, Yvonne f. 'Of all Breton names Yves is the commonest. It is the Old French nominative of Yvain, identical with Evan and John . . . From it are derived the female names Yvette and Yvonne' (Jack and Jill): **Yvette** from **Yves, Yvonne** from **Yvain.**

Z

Zachariah In Heb., 'God has remembered'.

Zachary A typical English simplification of **Zachariah.**

Zack, Zacky Diminutives of **Zachariah** and **Zachary.**

Zoë f., comes from Gr. zoë, 'life'. (Cf. **Eva.**) Pet-from : **Zo.**

Zona An American f. name; from Gr. for 'girdle'.

Zora derives from the Arabic for 'dawn'.